BOOKS BY KEN W. PURDY

THE WONDERFUL WORLD OF THE AUTOMOBILE

ALL BUT MY LIFE
with Stirling Moss

MOTORCARS OF THE GOLDEN PAST
with Tom Burnside

MOTORCARS OF THE GOLDEN PAST

Motorcars of the Golden Past

Text by Ken W. Purdy
Color Photographs by Tom Burnside

One Hundred Rare and Exciting Vehicles
from Harrah's Automobile Collection

GALAHAD BOOKS · NEW YORK CITY

Book Design: Michael Hampton

Text Copyright © 1965, 1966 by Ken W. Purdy
Photographs Copyright © 1966 by Tom Burnside

Library of Congress Catalog Card Number: 73-90837
ISBN 0-88365-138-6

Published by arrangement with Little, Brown and Company

Printed in the United States of America

Portions of the Introduction originally appeared in the Atlantic.

CONTENTS

MOTORCARS OF THE GOLDEN PAST

INTRODUCTION

Since the end of the Second World War, there has been a remarkable resurgence of interest in the automobile, not only as means of transportation, but as instrument of sport and as artifact. The biggest crowds that have assembled in Europe and in the United States for any purpose have come together to watch automobile racing, and museums dedicated to the preservation of the motorcar have sprung up all over the western world. Some of them are impressive. Probably as many as 250,000 people a year visit the Montagu Motor Museum at Beaulieu in England. The Daimler-Benz Museum in Stuttgart-Unterturkheim concentrates on the products of the oldest motorcar manufactory in the world, founded by the two men most frequently cited as the actual inventors of the automobile: Gottlieb Daimler and Karl Benz, who never met. The Museo dell' Automobile Carlo Biscaretti di Ruffia in Turin has an extraordinarily varied collection; Fritz Schlumpf of France plans to establish a museum to house his 160 specimens of a single make — the legendary Bugatti.

More collections existed in America during the 1940's and 1950's than there are now: the big James Melton and Cameron Peck collections have been broken up; the Pollard collection of Detroit is unrestored and unshown. In California, there is Briggs Cunningham's sizable collection. Brooks Stevens has a fine inventory of about 150 motorcars in Milwaukee. In the South there is the Stable of Thoroughbreds in Atlanta. But the biggest collection, and the finest, is in Reno, Nevada. William Harrah of Reno is the world's premier collector of automobiles. He has one thousand, give or take a few. (His master records may lag forty-eight hours or so behind the reports of his buying staff, so that he does not always know the exact census.) Harrah's purpose in amassing this astonishing number of motorcars is not mere acquisition. His is not the string-saver's compulsion, and, excepting two makes, Ford and Packard, he is not personally motivated.* His purpose is a plain one. It is to accumulate that number of automobiles that will, assembled under one roof, demonstrate, as nearly as it can be done, the history of the vehicle. No amount of money, no prodigies of effort, could accomplish Harrah's purpose. It is possible only to approach it, and it is the near-certainty that he will, of all collectors in our time, most nearly approach it, that distinguishes him.

A definitive collection of automobiles would have, for example, the steam tricycle of Nicholas Joseph Cugnot, built in France in 1771—and this his second model, the first being dated 1769. But it is in Paris, a

---

*For many years Harrah owned Fords and Packards in preference to other makes, and he thinks them both important in the history of the motorcar. He intends to own one of every year of each of the two makes. As this was written, he had acquired 97 Fords and 46 Packards. Partly because of this kind of duplication, the Harrah Collection favors U.S. over European cars by about 12 to 1.

national treasure housed in the Conservatoire Nationale des Arts et Metiers. It would have at least a model of the miniature steam car built between 1665 and 1680 by Fr. Ferdinand Verbiest, S.J., in China. It would have steam cars by Murdock and Trevithick and Gurney and Hancock, running in England as the nineteenth century came in. It would have Jean Joseph Etienne Lenoir's 1862–1863 car, which no longer exists, and Siegfried Markus's powered cart of 1865, which no longer exists, or his 1877 model, astonishingly foreshadowing today's automobiles — but that is held priceless by the Vienna Technical Museum, Markus having been Austrian.

So obsessed has man been with mechanical movement that the compilation of a full history of his invention would be a tremendous task: one would have to go from the appearance of the wheel, perhaps — who knows? — in India in 4000 B.C., to Mickey Thompson and the dragsters that do 200 miles an hour in a standing quarter-mile today.

Harrah still has about two hundred cars on his want list. His buyers are busily searching them out, while the rest of the staff, painters, upholsterers, mechanics, wheelwrights, look after those already on hand. The Harrah Collection occupies the full-time attention of a staff of 102.

Many cars come into the Collection's receiving department as basket cases, rusted, dented, broken after perhaps three decades under the leaky roof of a farm shed. Occasionally one may arrive under its own power. They may come, four at a time, in a huge Peterbilt diesel tractor-trailer rig, its sleeper cab fitted with the three bits of equipment that distinguish all Harrah regular-use cars: air-conditioning, fire extinguisher, seat belts. However a car looks on arrival, and some look very well indeed, it is not good enough to go on the floor of the No. 1 exhibition building in the complex that houses the Collection in Sparks, Nevada, just outside Reno. First it will be checked against factory specifications. The automotive library, housed in the main exhibition building, is the largest in private ownership. The staff can produce detailed specification sheets, blueprints, catalogues, magazine estimates and road tests on thousands of automobiles. Every car is checked. Perhaps an original Rochester carburetor has been changed for a Stromberg; the wheels are wearing the wrong size of tire; or three body-stripes are too close to each other by a millimeter. Researchers who are knowledgeable and intent will make a report, and the car will go to the shops. If it is a modern motorcar, and has been well cared for, it may be ready in a couple of weeks; if it's an antique, with wood framework rotted out, bodywork missing, its engine a lump of rust, it may be months in work.

Among old-car buffs, restoration is a term loosely

used. It may mean merely washing and polishing the car, daubing paint over any obvious rust-spots, and making the engine run somehow. In Great Britain cars wearing the original paint and upholstery are esteemed, and American methods are sometimes held to be vulgar, probably because they are not understood. To Harrah's technicians, a restored automobile is one that has been returned to the condition in which it left the factory. Under-restoration is thought unprofessional and slack; over-restoration is heinous. For example, steering-wheel spokes that were originally plated in nickel must not be done in chromium. That chromium is better-looking and easier to maintain is neither here nor there; nor does it matter that few visitors will be able to tell the difference. What matters are the original specifications. Harrah thinks no effort or expenditure excessive if it is necessary to establish an original specification. For example, he has paid $165 to make a set of 1928 Pierce-Arrow pedal-pads, although a mint set of 1929's was available, indistinguishable from the 1928's except by advanced experts. He does not think it unreasonable to spend weeks determining the exact construction methods and materials used for the interior of a door — and then seal the work off forever with upholstery. Harrah is obsessed with perfection, and so a screwhead is as important as a steering wheel. He sees no difference. Philip Frohman, architect of the National Cathedral in Washington, insisted that a molding 250 feet from the ground be moved by a fraction of an inch. From the floor, an expert with binoculars couldn't tell the difference, but Frohman couldn't understand why his action should be thought remarkable: the molding was in the wrong place; and he knew it. Therefore, it had imperatively to be moved.

When a car has been restored, it is tested on the road by Lee Jellison, a master mechanic who functions as Automotive Operations Manager, and by the General Manager of the Collection, Ralph Dunwoodie. If these two pass it, Harrah takes it on the road. He rejects as unsatisfactory and sends back for more work approximately fifty per cent of the cars. If there is something amiss, he will almost certainly find it.

He has watched the car in restoration and he knows every corner of it. "He sees, and holds in his hand," one of the mechanics told me, "every part that comes in here. Everything is spread out on a bench for him with a ticket showing where it came from and what it cost."

A "part" can be a set of rear springs for a 1912 Garford or a headlamp lens from a 1934 Cadillac. It can be anything from a bulb-horn to a custom-built touring body. Harrah's buyers are shrewd and indefatigable men. One room in one of the parts warehouses is solid with brass horns, headlights, sidelights, taillights. If a body-shop man needs a component part, 5 he can take it out of inventory, have it bought or have it made — and whether it's a mudguard brace or a complete "King of the Belgians" touring-car body doesn't really matter. When I was last in Reno, a replica pre–World War I Rolls-Royce body was being built. Finished, it will be indistinguishable from the original in every particular except one: Harrah's upholsterers can and do duplicate old diamond-pleating or any other kind of leatherwork, his wheelwrights can make a wooden wheel for a 1910 Palmer-Singer, and his painters could do 1910 coach-painting too, but they do not. The coach-painting technique was to lay down "ground coats" of color and cover them with many layers of clear varnish. The job took thirty days and lasted a year. Everyone uses modern paints today. Most collectors couldn't afford the old technique. Those who, like Harrah, can afford it in money can't afford it in time.

The income that enables William Harrah to consider reasonable an attempt to demonstrate the history of the automobile through one thousand perfectly conditioned, beautifully housed and lighted specimens, comes from the largest gaming establishment in the world, Harrah's Clubs in Reno and in Lake Tahoe, a few miles to the south on the California frontier. Like all Nevada gaming houses, they run twenty-four hours a day. Unlike many of the others, they run to near-capacity most of the time. Harrah runs the same games,

at the same house percentages, that other places run, but there is a startling difference in air, in tone. The root of the matter is shiny cleanliness and good taste. A marquee sign detailing the show-business acts with which all the big Nevada houses divert the client is lighted and moving — but only just: it's no jungle of neon or flashing bulbs, it's a big rectangle of opalescent white squares, moving slightly from side to side and so flickering in the back-light. It's better-looking by far than any other such come-on in town, and it probably pulls more business.

One enters Harrah's through a $40,000 air-door — it keeps out flies, warm air, all but determined dogs, and relieves the client of the necessity of so much as turning a knob. Within, the place shines. It is startlingly clean. The slot machines glitter. The felt surfaces of the crap tables obviously were vacuumed not long since. There are ashtrays everywhere — one in each slot machine, for example — and they are all empty, or they hold at most one cigarette butt. In the case of a major catastrophe — a dropped drink, for instance — a cleanup man will be on the scene within a minute, and probably sooner. There are square yards of mirror on the walls and ceiling, glistening like new ice. It is all Argus glass, one-way mirror. Behind it are galleries from which every foot of floor in the club can be observed, and in these galleries men sit at small tables with field glasses in their hands. They're looking for cheaters, for known criminals, for employees who do not smile and say thank you to the customers, and for dropped drinks and overflowing ashtrays as well. When Harrah came into Reno after the war, an unknown in the gaming world, he had three basic ideas: that a really successful gambling house would employ pleasant people who would run strictly honest games in a surgically clean atmosphere. On this system he has prospered, to state the matter mildly. Since Harrah's is privately held, public disclosure of profit-and-loss is not required. The closest anyone who knows will come to disclosing Harrah's income is the term the Rolls-Royce people always use when asked the horsepower of their cars: "It is adequate." Harrah's income is adequate for many purposes, even if those purposes include the maintenance of one thousand motorcars. The Collection is a traffic-builder for Harrah's Club and contributes substantially to its own support: admission is one dollar, refundable at Harrah's Club in Reno if presented within twenty-four hours.

The just-washed, shiny-bright tone that marks the gaming rooms obtains everywhere over the five acres that house the Harrah Collection. There are separate shops for sandblasting, for steam-cleaning and washing, for bodywork, for upholstering, and they are all as nearly spotless as possible. The main restoration shop, housed in the same building with the executive offices, the library and the best of the cars, looks like a small demonstration factory: machine shop, massive overhead electric hoists, soft fluorescent lighting. A dozen projects are simultaneously in hand. Three mechanics are rebuilding a Stutz Bearcat, one of the earlier, bucket-seat models, a bright buttercup yellow. Every part they are working with has been painted or polished, there is nothing in sight that would stain a white glove. Next to them a young man, wearing a cinnamon-brown pointed beard, is striping a 1913 popcorn wagon. He does striping only, and he will work on the wagon from ten in the morning until five the next morning. There is a big rush on it, as there is on the Stutz: both must be ready for a major meeting of the Nevada Horseless Carriage Club in a few days. The popcorn wagon, which Harrah's buyers found in California, is red and white, rich with cut glass, extensible awnings, frosted light bulbs. The striper's long knife-blade brush is laying on red, gold and black. The wagon has been rebuilt inside and out. The cabinet-makers have made new shelves and drawers of oak; the tiny steam engine, without which no popcorn wagon could claim to be the real thing, has been seen to by a specialist steam-mechanic. When the striper has finished restoring the original pattern of straight lines and curlicues, the wagon will be ready to roll out and open for business, except for one thing: a frosted glass panel cites for sale "Popcorn and Crisps." The research department people have not yet discovered what "crisps" were in 1913. Opinions vary: crisps were potato chips, or they were corn chips, or they were something else altogether. Never mind, there will be an adequate supply of veritable 1913 crisps in the popcorn wagon when the little steam engine begins to spin, no one doubts that.

A pair of Rolls-Royces, a Doble steamer, a long-chassis Duesenberg, a stretch-out Cadillac bus from Yosemite Park, a Thomas . . . mechanics and artisans work on them behind a protective line of finished cars, and signs enjoin tourists not to question the help. Nearly always in family groups, the sightseers pass on into the main exhibition room, with many a murmur, "They don't make 'em like that any more!"

This building was a railroad icing plant handling the long expresses running East out of the Pacific coast fruit-growing country. It is high-ceilinged and huge, lined with cork slabs from top to bottom. The near-obsession with neatness and detail that marks Harrah operations shows everywhere: the aisles are marked off not by dust-catching fabric ropes, but by transparent plastic tubing, and the supporting posts are topped by small ashtrays. A commentator-guard mounts an observation platform high in the center of the room. He answers questions, directs the tourists, and suggests strongly that they keep their hands off the automobiles. He is bored but competent. He is well paid. The room is air-conditioned and pleasant. At lunchtime he'll go to the employees' cafeteria, a clean, well-lighted place. (At least once, every time I have been there, a man has come by to polish the glass in the front door.) The food is good, the servings big, the prices under the market. There is a low turnover among Harrah's employees. His tendency is to think well of people. He loathes being cheated out of money, time, work or anything else, but otherwise . . . A watchman in one of his two Reno garages tells of a Sunday afternoon when Harrah came in and asked him how he felt. The man said he was a little on edge, there was nothing to do, nothing happening.

"Why don't you get in the back of the brown Rolls-Royce and turn on the television?" Harrah said.

He wouldn't think of it, the watchman said.

"Oh, go ahead, get in," Harrah said. "You can still see the door from there."

Harrah is a tall, lean, graying man in his early fifties. He has a soft voice and speaks infrequently and then, usually, shortly. One night, in Tahoe, listening to the great mechanical clatter of hundreds of slot machines under busy play, I said to him:

"Bill, that is the sound of madness."

"No," he said, "it isn't."

"It is," I said.

"You wouldn't say that," Harrah said, "if they were your slots." He is a good listener in the sense that he absorbs everything that is said around him, but he rarely looks directly at the speaker or appears to pay close attention. He seems to be withdrawn, distant, preoccupied, but he is wholly courteous. He doesn't smoke or drink and he eats little. He seems to gamble, that is, to play from the other side of the table, only ritually, although he says he enjoys it. He goes to Las Vegas to gamble, as a matter of convention does not play in Reno, and he plays to a limit, say $1200. If he loses that, he's through for the night. He does not appear to be inscrutable, or hard, or calculating, or anything else that is cliché about his profession, although obviously, on the evidence, he is all these things. He travels in Europe a good deal, but he says he likes Reno and would rather live there than anywhere else he knows. His home, white, modern, set in lawns unusually green for Nevada, is ten minutes from his office. His wife is a tall, pretty woman, blonde. Her air is bland and tranquil. The Harrahs have no children. When they travel by motorcar, most frequently to Lake Tahoe and back, they go separately, and they drive very fast. Nevada has no speed limits on open roads, and people buzzing along at 75 are often surprised to be passed by, say, a Ferrari and a Bentley Continental running together 50 miles an hour faster. Fast driving is important to the Harrahs. Neither of them would think 95 MPH really hurrying. They willingly accept the ordinary hazards of speed, but they do not propose being hurt by avoidable accident. Mrs.

Harrah's favorite car at the moment is a 150-MPH Ferrari 2+2, one of the sturdiest and safest motorcars being built today, but it is put on a lift and given at least a cursory check every time it runs the 110 miles to Tahoe and back. Harrah doesn't care for overexposure to chance. He began learning to fly, at fifty-one, because he often travels in chartered aircraft, and it seemed absurd to him that his life should be dependent on the life of only one other man. He can take over and land the ordinary light plane now, and he thinks he'll go on to twin-engine instrument rating. He has begun to collect historic airplanes. He is interested in railroads, too; he has one narrow-gauge locomotive, and he plans to set up three miles or so of track around the Collection in the future. He runs a 53-foot cruiser on Lake Tahoe (it has two Allison engines and is very fast, over 50 miles an hour). He owns two unlimited class hydroplanes, single-seat racing boats that will do around 180 miles an hour.

His primary interest remains the automobile. Three years ago, in explaining that interest, he said, "Few material things have been as important to America as the automobile. The manufacture of the automobile was the root of our industrial growth, and for decades now it has been the central support of our economy. We are all tied to the automobile by history, by business, by emotion. The automobile deserves to be preserved and remembered."

9

De DION-BOUTON

Year: *1899*
Model: *Not designated*
Cylinders: *1*
Horsepower: *2¼*
Price: *$400*

Le Comte Albert de Dion was a significant figure in the *haute monde* of Paris in the 1880's, a dandy, a gourmet, a ladies' man, and a gentleman much interested in everything happening in the world around him. The significant fact of life in the 1880's was the emergence of mechanical locomotion, and De Dion was struck, one day, by the excellence of some toy steam engines by two modelmakers named Bouton and Trepardoux. De Dion set them up in a little shop and told them to make a steam carriage. The first one ran in 1883. Unlike most contemporary steam vehicles, which ran to locomotive proportions, it was quite light. Still, it was not light enough, and De Dion and Bouton became convinced that steam engines would always be too heavy. They elected to try gasoline. Trepardoux dissented, and left De Dion's employ.

Georges Bouton now made a very small (135 cubic centimeters or so) single-cylinder engine. He intended it to run slowly, as engines were supposed to do then, but it would work well only at such incredible rates as 3000 RPM. Bouton worked out an ignition system that would fire at 1500 and soon realized that he had in his hand the world's first successful high-speed internal combustion engine. It went into the first De Dion–Bouton tricycle, in 1895, a vehicle intended to do perhaps 20 miles an hour, and to climb mild hills with the assistance of the driver's weight on the pedals. Merely *pour le sport*, De Dion–Bouton entered five of these trikes in the Paris-Marseilles-Paris automobile race of 1896. Three finished, and one was third overall! Engine size was increased until, in September 1899, a De Dion–Bouton tricycle actually won the Paris-Ostend automobile race, doing 201 miles at an average of nearly 33 miles an hour. In the same year, finding the trikes becoming heavy and unwieldy, De Dion–Bouton began to make four-wheel vehicles, using on them the ingenious "De Dion rear drive," in which a dead axle carries the wheels, with the power separately applied through two universal-jointed shafts. The De Dion system has been used on some very advanced high-performance and racing cars in modern times.

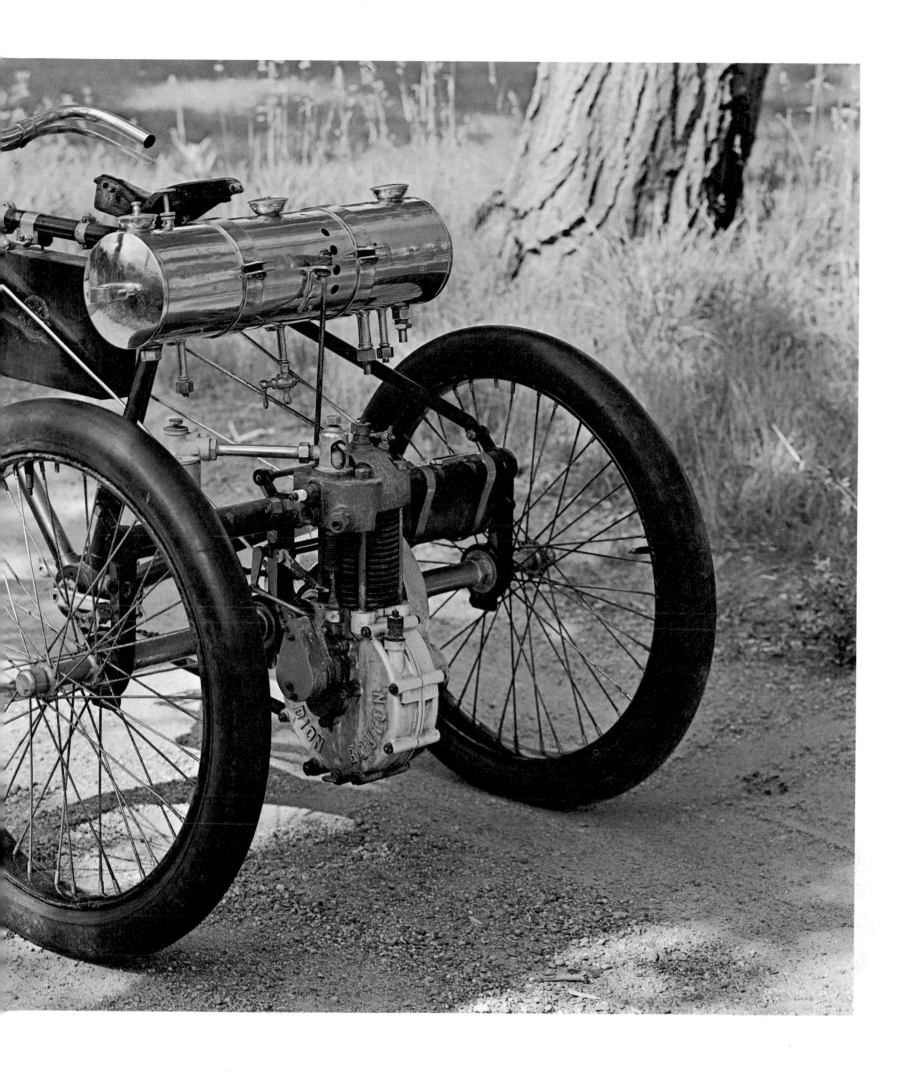

WINTON

Year: *1900*
Model: *Not designated*
Cylinders: *1*
Horsepower: *9*
Price: *$1200*

On April 1, 1898, the first Winton was sold, and it is a disputant for the title of the first American motorcar to go across the counter. It was said to have had the first U.S.–made pneumatic tires, at $100 each. But the Scots mechanic who made it is secure in immortality on two other counts. It was Alexander Winton who put the Packard brothers into the business by sneering at James Packard, come to complain that his Winton didn't go like a Winton should, "If you're so smart, why don't you build a better car yourself?" And the fact that he could beat the great Winton driving his famed "Bullet" did much to convince Henry Ford that he was as good as he thought he might be. They raced on frozen Lake St. Claire, north of Detroit.

Winton's early one-cylinder cars, like this one, were tiller-steered, a system that has much to recommend it. Wheel steering is certainly archaic and can't be expected to last more than another decade or two. Such evolutionary changes show up soonest on racing cars, and the steering wheel has already begun to look like a

vestigial appendage on European grand prix automobiles, with diameters under 12 inches common. Modified tiller or crossbar steering makes much more sense than wheel steering when steering is easy and great mechanical advantage is not needed.

Winton was involved in one of the louder and more amusing controversies of the pre–Kaiser War period, when one of his customers, a Dr. H. Nelson Jackson, in 1903 drove a standard Winton touring car across the country. When anonymous competitors circulated stories to the effect that the good doctor had gone part of the way by freight train, the Winton company offered $10,000 for proof, and, when no one tried for it, was emboldened to raise the ante to $25,000. No one came forward for that, either.

Winton stopped production of automobiles in 1924, when he was making big tourers and sedans and limousines of excellent quality, and changed over to industrial diesel engines. General Motors bought him out in 1930.

DARRACQ

Year: *1901*
Model: *B1*
Cylinders: *1*
Horsepower: *6*
Price: *$960*

Alexandre Darracq was known all his life as a shrewd fellow, a hard man to do out of a *sou*. Trained as a draftsman, he went into bicycle manufacture in the 1890's, and became a kind of two-wheeler tycoon. He sold out to a British outfit, accepting, as part of the deal, a stipulation that he should not make any more bicycles. He made parts for bicycles, and another fortune doing it.

When the idea of motor-propelled two- and three- and four-wheeled vehicles began to loom large on the horizon in France, the country that was for years to be the world leader in automobilism, Darracq did not propose to stand aside. He put a motorcycle-like device on the market. It was extraordinary in design, driven by a rear-mounted engine of rotary configuration and no fewer than five cylinders! It did not as-

tonish the world. By 1895, Darracq was making small four-wheel vehicles, again without creating any sensations. Unlike most manufacturers of his day, Darracq was not concerned with making big luxury cars; he had had an early glimpse of the Ford-Austin vision, and wanted to make small, cheap machines. By the year 1900, he had a fair 6½-horsepower car in production, at the rate of roughly a hundred a month. These were soundly designed, well-made cars, with the bonnet-line that later characterized Renault and Franklin cars. The two-cylinder 12-horsepower car of 1901 became one of the best-known old cars in the world, when it appeared in the film *Genevieve*.

Darracq retired a millionaire before the Kaiser War. The firm ran on until 1919, when it merged with Talbot.

14

OLDSMOBILE

Year: *1902*
Model: *R*
Cylinders: *1*
Horsepower: *4–6*
Price: *$700*

Ransom Eli Olds was among the company of pioneers in American auto-building. When he was eighty he was asked what had brought him into the business. His answer was short and honest. "I didn't like the smell of horses," he said.

Living in Lansing, Michigan, working in his father's machine shop, R. E. Olds had built a couple of buggy-based automobiles by 1895. He acquired some financial backing in 1899 and formed the Olds Motor Works in Detroit. This was the first factory designed from scratch to make automobiles. All the others had been converted from some other purpose. Here the one-cylinder Curved-Dash Oldsmobile was built. It was not the first product. The first one was a big, and, for the time, an expensive car, selling for $1250, and it failed. Olds decided to add to his line a car costing half that, and designed the Curved-Dash. At about this time, most fortuitously, the factory burned flat, and nothing was saved except the pilot model of the little car—and it

only because an office employee ran into the fire and pushed it out. The idea of making anything else was abandoned, the Curved-Dash became the top of the Oldsmobile line, and the first quantity-produced American car. It was a good one, too, with tiller steering, two speeds forward, one reverse. It cost $650 and by 1903 sales totaled around 3750. That was a third of all the motorcars sold that year in this country. The Curved-Dash ran on until 1907 in the original form, but a two-cylinder came out in 1905 and a four-cylinder car in 1906. R. E. Olds had left the company by then, in 1904, when a quarrel with his board of directors resulted in serious loss of confidence all around. He started the Reo company the same year. In 1908 the Olds Motor Works was sucked up into General Motors, and is still a potent force in the GM structure. A good many of the original cars survive; in 1964 the Curved-Dash club mustered forty of them for a parade in New York.

18

HAYNES-APPERSON

Year: *1902*
Model: *Not designated*
Cylinders: *2*
Horsepower: *6*
Price: *$1200*

Kokomo, Indiana, as unlikely-sounding a place as can be found south of Oshkosh, was the home of Elmer and Edgar Apperson, mechanics, aged thirty-one and twenty-four years on the day in October 1893 when Elwood Haynes, a metallurgist, told them he had a one-cylinder gasoline engine that he thought could be made to run a buggy. The Appersons said they'd give it a try, or, rather, Elmer said they would. He was the boss. He turned the job over to Edgar and told Haynes what it would cost him: 40 cents an hour, and they'd get to it when they could.

Eight months later, on the third of July, the first gasoline automobile the Appersons had ever seen, the first Haynes-Apperson, was ready, and it ran on the Fourth, after it had been towed out into the countryside behind a horse and buggy, to avoid the celebrating crowds in Kokomo. It ran without argument, at around 10 or 12 miles an hour. A quarter of a century later, taken out of the Smithsonian Institution by Elwood Haynes, it still ran, leading a parade up Broadway in New York. The Haynes-Apperson had three speeds forward, a differential, a foot throttle, a thermo-syphon cooling system for its two-horsepower engine.

For the next car, Apperson built everything, including the engine, two cylinders opposed, on the principle that Porsche uses today. This car was entered in the famous Chicago *Herald* race of 1895, but dropped a front wheel into a streetcar track and broke it before the race started. The Haynes-Apperson company was formed in 1898 and made and sold a dozen cars. Clearly showing its buggy ancestry—Edgar Apperson had put a body on the steel frame of the first car, and out of whimsy, had left the whipsocket on it—the Haynes-Apperson was nevertheless a going automobile, and took its share of notice in the competitions that served as advertising in those days, some of them minor wonders that caused strong men to marvel: running for 100 miles without a stop over mud roads in the rain, for instance.

In 1901, Edgar Apperson resigned and he and Elmer set up shop under their own name. Forty years later, his friend, the writer Robert Pinkerton, asked Edgar why he had quit. "Because I was getting twenty dollars a week," Apperson said.

PANHARD-LEVASSOR

Year: *1902*
Model: *B1*
Cylinders: *4*
Horsepower: *15*
Price: *$6000*

Emile Levassor and René Panhard were Paris tool-makers who, quite naturally, saw the great Exhibition of 1889, and Gottlieb Daimler's quadricycle motor vehicle. Levassor had the audacity to think he could do better, if he could lay hands on Daimler's engine, and this, through his friend, Edouard Sarazin, he was able to do; in fact Panhard-Levassor were licensed to build Daimler engines in France.

The 1890/91 Panhard-Levassor is often called the first true automobile. The authority J. D. Scheel says, in effect, that it marks "the dividing line between the horse-drawn carriage and the motorcar." Levassor laid out the components as they have nearly always been laid out ever since: engine in front, clutch, gearbox, driveshaft, differential on the rear axle.

A Panhard-Levassor won the first true motor race in Europe, and perhaps in the world, in 1895, run from Paris to Bordeaux and back, 732 miles. Emile Levassor himself drove almost the whole way, except for a few kilometers uphill, when he let his riding mechanic have the tiller. He was on the road for 53 hours, and running for 48 hours and 48 minutes! He had averaged a hair under 15 miles an hour for the whole distance, running at night under candle-burning headlamps. Back in Paris, he had a cup of bouillon, poached eggs and two glasses of champagne. He did not appear to be at all fatigued. *Un pilote formidable*, to say the least. Until 1902, Panhard cars pretty much controlled racing in Europe. In 1909 they adopted the Knight sleeve-valve engine, always more popular in Europe than in the United States, where it had been invented: Daimler, Rover, Minerva and Mercedes also used it.

After the Hitler War, Panhard put out a two-cylinder air-cooled car, designed by the noted front-wheel-drive expert J. A. Gregoire. The Dyna-Panhard, in its own right and as the Deutsch-Bonnet and Panhard-Monopole, dominated its class (501–750 cc.) and the Index of Performance at Le Mans in the 1950's.

PACKARD

Year: *1903*
Model: *F*
Cylinders: *1*
Horsepower: *12*
Price: *$2500*

The Packard brothers, James Ward and William Dowd, first thought of making a motorcar in 1893. They had the means. They lived in a town in Ohio, Warren, named after their father, Warren Packard; the family owned prospering businesses and extensive real estate. James Ward Packard, a university-trained mechanical engineer, returning from a trip to Europe, brought a De Dion–Bouton tricycle with him. In August 1898, he bought Winton No. 12, the dozenth car built by the great Alexander Winton, in Cleveland, fifty miles from Warren. It couldn't make the distance under its own power, and Packard came home behind a team of horses. It was this that led to the famous confrontation between Packard and Winton, ending with Packard's *riposte* to Winton's suggestion that he build a car of his own, if he was so all-fired smart: "You know, Mr. Winton, I think I will." He hired a couple of Winton associates, W. A. Hatcher and George L. Weiss, set up a workshop in the electrical plant of a summer hotel the family owned, and went to work.

On November 6, 1899, the first Packard ran on the streets of Warren. Like so many other pioneer cars, it looked like a buggy that had lost its horses, but it was no primitive: it had three forward speeds, and, of all things, an automatic spark advance. They sold it for $1250. The following year, Packard made a sensational debut at the New York Automobile Show in Madison Square Garden. Three were sold in five days, one of them to a Rockefeller. The company was little prepared for the popularity which fell to it, and James Ward Packard had to answer a request for literature by ordering his secretary to write the man: "Tell him we don't have any literature. Tell him to ask the man who owns one!" By 1901, Packard gears were being shifted through the industry's first H-slot pattern, and the Packards were the first production-line machines to standardize on wheel steering. In 1903, the famous one-cylinder Packard "Old Pacific" (identical with this Harrah car) made a 3500-mile coast-to-coast run in sixty-one days after thirty futile attempts by other machines had been racked up. In 1904 the racer "Gray Wolf" broke the national one-mile record thirteen times in two days and the Packard Company was off and running.

WHITE

Year: *1904*
Model: *D*
Cylinders: *2*
Horsepower *10*
Price *$2150*

Second longest-lived of all the steamers, the White of Cleveland was for a time one of the most talked-about automobiles made in the United States. It was made by a sewing-machine company, indeed the second biggest sewing-machine company in the world, and made an overnight reputation on the race tracks. A weird-looking machine, a kind of pointed box on a set of wheels, the White was entered in a 10-mile race at the Detroit Fair Grounds and turned it into a joke. Photographs of the White racer show it all by itself— the other cars, gasoline-powered for the most part, are nowhere in sight. Sent to Great Britain, to compete in a Reliability Run over a course of 650 miles, in a field of seventy entrants, the White was one of two finishers to set up a perfect score. The company was sharp and progressive, cataloguing, as early as 1903, automatic engine lubrication and two independently functioning sets of brakes. A delivery truck on the White chassis appeared the same year, and a luxury limousine the following year. Unlike the Stanley, and most other steamers, the White interposed a clutch between engine and road wheels, so that the engine could idle at stops if the driver wished.

In 1905, the famous "Whistling Billy" White racing car began to storm the tracks. Driver Jay Webb and "Whistling Billy" (after the sound of its exhaust steam) became, like Barney Oldfield and his "Blitzen Benz," one of the headline clichés of the day. The combination constantly beat, or harried to the finish line by a second or so, cars costing three and four times as much, and for a time held the world record for a mile track at 74.07 MPH. White steamers were steady high-rank finishers in the Glidden Tours, and Walter C. White himself drove in the Vanderbilt Cup. President Theodore Roosevelt had a White, and in 1908, a White ran away with the San Francisco Hillclimb, a humiliating 16 seconds faster than the quickest gasoline automobile. But, good as it was, the White was still a steamer, with all a steamer's faults: weight, slow starting, great thirst for water, boiler-maintenance problems; and in 1910, the farsighted White management went over to gasoline.

26

KNOX

Year: *1904*
Model: *Tudor*
Cylinders: *2*
Horsepower: *20*
Price: *$2400*

This Knox touring car ran in the 1962 London-to-Brighton Run, held every autumn to celebrate the abolition of anti-automobile legislation in November 1896. Harrah drove the car.

Harry Knox began in 1900 and his early vehicles were known as Knox "Waterless" automobiles. He worked out an uncommon system of heat-radiation: 1750 two-inch-long pins were screwed into the cylinder walls, in a hedgehog effect, to such purpose, Knox said, that he had 32 square inches of cooling surface for every single square inch of cylinder wall. Nevertheless, in later years Knox abandoned air-cooling for liquid.

"Made in America for Americans" was Knox's chauvinistic tag-line for his first car, a 1901 tricycle, tiller-steered, air-cooled, single-cylindered. Like the Davis of which so much was heard around 1948 — and so little afterward — the Knox's single wheel was in front, an arrangement usually held to make for instability, but perhaps not at the speeds of which the 8-horsepower trike was capable. Price was $750, and Knox, who made nearly everything in the car himself, including sparkplugs and ball bearings, said it would do 30 miles to the gallon carrying two people.

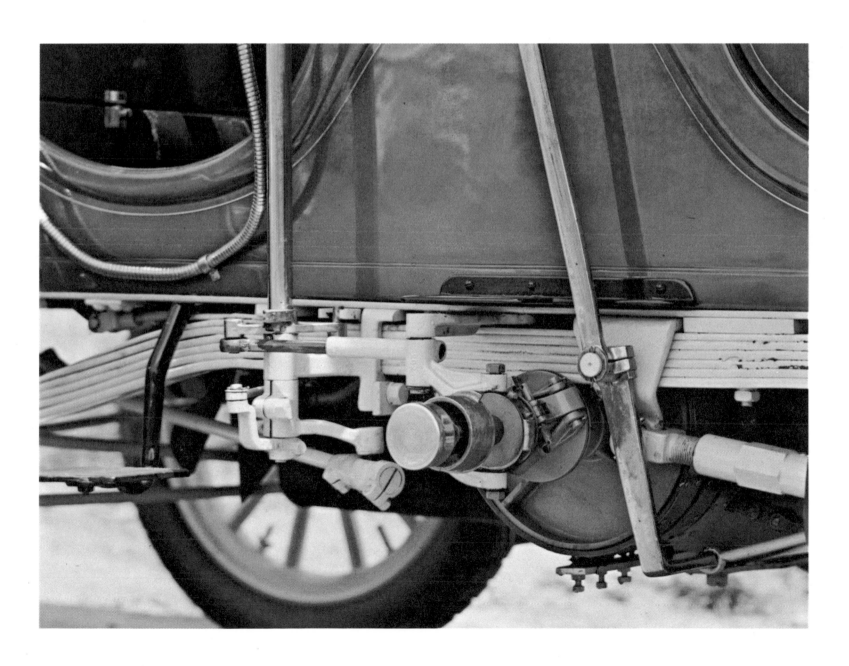

PEERLESS *+ MORS FROM FRANCE*

Year: *1905*
Model: *11*
Cylinders: *4*
Horsepower: *35*
Price: *$4000*

In 1899, 1900 and 1901 three motorcars of the first quality came on the scene, in Detroit, Cleveland and Buffalo: the Packard, the Peerless, the Pierce-Arrow. They were held to be co-equals: luxurious, beautifully built, fast and expensive. The Peerless, in the years 1904–1908, was a name as familiar to racing devotees as Ferrari is today, for those were the days of the Peerless "Green Dragon" and the all-conquering Berner Eli "Barney" Oldfield. Oldfield, a bicycle racer, had been contracted by Henry Ford to drive his "999" and he handled the famous Winton "Bullet" too. Louis Mooers of Peerless, an impressive figure whose career was sadly short, hired Oldfield to drive the Green Dragon, a monster with cylinders of six inches bore and stroke. Before Peerless stopped racing in 1908, Oldfield held every circular track record from one mile to fifty. He once broke twelve records in two days. He wrecked the first Green Dragon and Mooers built him another.

This four-cylinder Model 11 Peerless touring car was produced at the height of the company's racing fame. As time went on, the car was brought up to an extraordinary pitch of refinement. Such niceties as a crankshaft ground from the solid billet, pistons and piston rings polished and lapped, connecting rods weighed to gram tolerances, the entire engine balanced, and so on, were standard practice. Peerless offered a self-starter in 1913, the year after Cadillac's, and it was an amazing device. It would start the engine with the car in gear: a Peerless weighing 5100 pounds was driven 660 feet up a 7 per cent grade in 12 minutes on the starter alone, without exhausting the battery.

Peerless made a V–8 in 1915 and had some success with it, but the car deteriorated badly in the 1920's until in 1929 the company hired the designer Alexis de Sahknoffsky to do the 1930 line. Sahknoffsky's cars were lovely. Attempting to stay with the multicylinder trend of the times, Peerless designed a V–16 for 1931, both engine and body—by Walter Murphy, who was to do so many bodies for Duesenberg—making extensive use of aluminum. However, only three V–16's were made, and but one is known to exist today. The company went out of business in 1932.

POPE-TOLEDO

Year: *1906*
Model: *R-XII*
Cylinders: *4*
Horsepower: *45*
Price: *$3700*

Colonel Albert A. Pope gave his name to a number of automobiles: the Pope-Hartford, Pope-Toledo, Pope-Tribune, Pope-Waverly, Pope-Robinson. He had been head of the Pope Manufacturing Company of Hartford, Connecticut, important bicycle-makers, and, when the automobile boom began to appear in the distant future, he put the firm into the manufacture of an electric automobile. (He then wanted nothing to do with steam or, particularly, gasoline engines, on the grounds that the public would be afraid of them.) This aspect of Pope's interests—it was called the Motor Carriage Department—was bought out around 1900 by the Electric Vehicle Company, an outfit that was attempting to erect a monopoly in electric road-transport, in the belief that steam and gasoline would fail. By 1907, the Electric Vehicle Company was bankrupt, having guessed spectacularly wrongly, but in the safe was U. S. Patent 549,160 of November 5, 1895, which gave to George B. Selden of Rochester, New York, complete protection on the *invention* of the gasoline-powered motorcar. Electric Vehicle had bought it for $10,000 and a fifth of anything it made. From then until 1911, when Henry Ford, fighting alone and at great cost, broke it in the courts, the Selden Patent cost every U.S. car-maker 1¼ per cent of the price of every car he made, a levy that totaled in the millions.

Salesmen of this Toledo-made Pope boasted that it developed one horsepower for every 54 pounds of weight, would do nearly 16 miles to the gallon of gasoline, and had final-drive sprockets that could quickly be changed to alter the gear ratio if extra power were needed for steep hills or muddy roads.

COMPOUND

Year: *1906*
Model: *7½*
Cylinders: *3*
Horsepower: *16*
Price: *$1300*

This Compound Light Touring Car is a most unusual mechanical curiosity. The engine is gasoline-powered, but runs on the principle common to compound steam engines, which use high-pressure steam in one cylinder or pair of cylinders, then pass it as exhaust into a low-pressure cylinder or pair. In the Compound, the two primary cylinders, of 4-inch stroke and 4-inch bore, exhaust into a bigger cylinder set between them, this one of 7-inch bore and 4-inch stroke. This cylinder runs solely on the pressure of exhaust gas from the other two. The engine is very quiet, since most of the exhaust noise is absorbed by the middle cylinder. The exhaust is startlingly cool, too.

The Compound was a Connecticut car, made in Middletown, and the design was by John Unser. He had another original notion: a power-brake mechanism, operating on pressure from a small engine-driven air pump. This was a "deadman's switch" arrangement: the weight of the driver's right arm held it closed. If the driver lifted his arm, either because he was dropping dead or waving to a friend, the brakes went on.

ADAMS-FARWELL

Year: *1906*
Model: *7-A*
Cylinders: *5*
Horsepower: *40/45*
Price: *$2750*

The air-cooling of internal-combustion engines has always been an initially attractive proposition. It was particularly attractive in pioneer times in cold countries, when the problem of wintertime freeze-ups was serious. Most manufacturers, an eye on airplane and motorcycle practice, have settled on the convention of wreathing ordinary in-line cylinders in fins (the Knox Waterless used a hedgehog arrangement of pins instead) and arranging for the airstream to blow over them when the car is moving fast, a fan to take care of things when it's stationary or slow. The designers of the Adams-Farwell, a vehicle the production of which enlivened industrial circles in Dubuque, Iowa, from 1904 until 1913, went rather farther: they made a radial engine, its three or five cylinders set in a circle, and, not satisfied even with that departure from convention, they made it a rotary.

A rotary engine is a spinning engine, that is to say, the engine itself turns, and the crankshaft is stationary, instead of the other way around. The best known rotaries have been aircraft engines, the Le Rhone Gnome and Clerget and Bentley rotaries of the First World War. In these, the propeller was bolted directly to the engine and the whole works revolved as a unit. Except for a tendency to throw oil all over the place, to run hot and cold unevenly, and to kill pilots who forgot to make low-altitude climbing turns *against* the engine's direction of turn, not with it, they worked well enough.

On the Adams-Farwell, the engine lived in the rear, underneath the seat, spun in a horizontal plane and drove a chain through a planetary transmission. There were four speeds forward, plus reverse. Steering was by tiller, and all this novelty cost about 2750 of the dollars of the period, which were larger in every way than ours.

REO

Year: *1906*
Model: *M*
Cylinders: *2*
Horsepower: *16*
Price: *$2000*

Reo of course stands for R. E. Olds, who made the Oldsmobile and left that firm in 1904, after a dispute with his directors over a policy matter: the desirability of making big or small cars. The Reo company was to make automobiles from 1904 to 1936. This Model M was called a Depot Wagon, and the customer was assured that it was equipped with every appointment and convenience known to the trade. The tall, square, closed body was interchangeable, after the fashion of the time, with an open touring body, the engine was a two-cylinder horizontally opposed device offering two forward speeds and one in reverse, top speed about 25 miles an hour.

Ransom Olds was more than a builder, he had a marked flair for publicity, and some of his promotions are well remembered. For instance, in 1907 he was advertising that a Reo Runabout had run 57 miles on one and three-quarters gallons of gasoline — "the rain was coming down in sheets" — while carrying four people, and had also lugged the same four people 682 miles for an expenditure of $3.38 each. The year before he had made an exact replica, on a big-toy scale, of the two-cylinder Reo touring car, a working model with a compressed-air engine. This enchanting little device would carry four children, and the Barnum & Bailey Circus bought it and made it a feature of every performance, with a cargo of four adults — adult midgets. Olds could be counted on to furnish cars or trucks for any purpose that promised worthwhile publicity: a Reo truck, the name prominent on its side, carried spare tires for the 1911 Glidden Tour participants. In 1912, Olds ran a famous advertisement, one sometimes cited as comparable with Cadillac's "The Penalty of Leadership" and Ned Jordan's "Somewhere West of Laramie." It was headed "The Car That Marks My Limit" and told a breathless world that the model Reo the Fifth, selling at $1055, was in Olds's considered opinion the best automobile it was possible to build. Indeed, he said, he thought it came "pretty close to finality." "I call it," he said, "My Farewell Car."

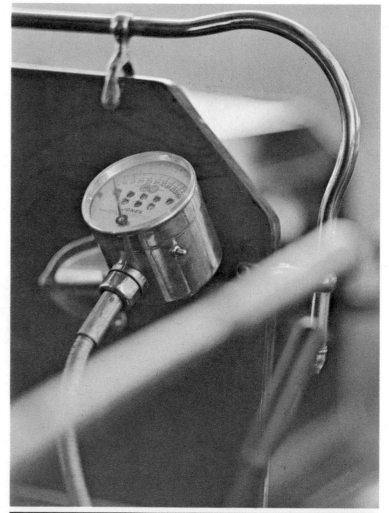

LOZIER

Year: *1906*
Model: *D*
Cylinders: *4*
Horsepower: *40*
Price: *$5500*

H. A. Lozier was an obsessed perfectionist type of pioneer, and he made some of the best motorcars that ran the roads during the first two decades of the twentieth century. Lozier was a marine-engine manufacturer, but he wasn't much interested in workboats; his were high-speed racing engines, known all over the world as among the best. In 1902, he decided to try automobiles, and sent one of his engineers to France, then the hub of the motorcar industry, to see what the standards were. Very high, the man reported. Lozier did not feel they were too high to be exceeded. He believed in quality over cost, and he was always willing to experiment. For example, in 1907 he attacked the problem of brake heat-dissipation by water-cooling the drums, which were channeled. The water was delivered from a supply tank, under air pressure, at the driver's volition. The idea was still so appealing in the 1950's that Briggs Cunningham tried it on one of his Le Mans cars. Lozier simplified the problem of restarting on a hill, tricky in the days of heavy clutches,

straight-tooth gears and hand-cranked engines, by building a pawl-and-ratchet into his brake system. With the pawl engaged, at the driver's discretion, the car could move forward, but backward running was mechanically impossible. Lozier made one of the first all-ball-and-roller-bearing engines, too — expensive, but in its time, when babbitt bearings were crude and short-lived, pleasantly efficient.

Lozier race cars were, naturally enough in the light of the quality standards enforced, formidable competitors. When 450 miles of the first Indianapolis 500 Race had been run, a Lozier was well ahead, and appeared certain of winning until a slow pit crew put it out of contention. In the same year, the great Teddy Tetzlaff took on Ralph de Palma in a 100-mile match race and beat him by 6 miles! Tetzlaff was driving a 46-horsepower Lozier, De Palma a Fiat of just twice that rating.

This touring car, the oldest Lozier known, was found in the town of Truth or Consequences, New Mexico.

PACKARD

Year: *1907*
Model: *30*
Cylinders: *4*
Horsepower: *30*
Price: *$5600*

The first man to drive his family across the United States used a Packard 30, and made the trip in a bit over 32 days. Much of it has been forgotten now, but in its day, the Packard had a great mystique, and many were the wild stories told of it. Some of them were true. The oil-rich Osage Indians of Oklahoma were the counterparts of today's Arabian sheiks, and one chief was said to have bought a Packard for spot cash and phoned, an hour later, from a town 65 miles away,

to say that he had smashed it and wanted another immediately. Harry K. Thaw, central figure in one of the great scandals of the years before the Kaiser War (he killed the celebrated architect Stanford White) used a Packard in his subsequent escape from the Matteawan Insane Asylum. The Packard house organ felt entitled to comment: "When high speed is necessary, when a fast getaway is absolutely imperative, ask the man who owns one."

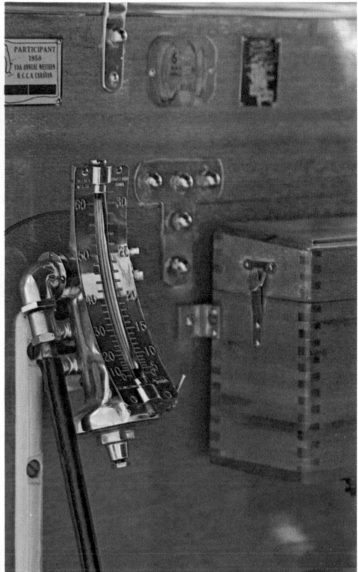

THOMAS

Year: *1907*
Model: *35*
Cylinders: *4*
Horsepower: *70*
Price: *$4500*

The New York-to-Paris race of 1908 covered 21,000 miles and this is the car that won it: a Thomas Flyer. The Harrah Collection acquired it from Henry Austin Clark, Jr., and it has been restored, as nearly as possible, to the exact condition in which it ran the 170-day race. The man who drove the car, George Schuster, came to Reno to see it again in the summer of 1964 (he was ninety-two then) and attested it. After the car had been restored, William Harrah drove it to the 14,110-foot summit of Pikes Peak.

The New York-to-Paris race was inspired by the Paris-Peking race of the year before, 1907, comparatively a short run at 8000 miles. It had been won by Prince Scipione Borghese of Italy in an Itala. There were six entries for the New York-to-Paris: a German Protos, a De Dion–Bouton, a Sizaire-Naudin and a Motobloc from France, an Italian Zust, and the Thomas. The foreign entries had been very carefully prepared and modified. For example, the De Dion–Bouton's driver had run in the Paris-Peking, it had a heater, then a great novelty, it carried steel-studded Michelin tires and flanged wheels to be run on railway tracks. The Protos had been built to Prussian standards by men who knew they were working in Kaiser Wilhelm's personal interest. The Sizaire-Naudin was driven by a Paris-Peking veteran. Six days before the start, there was no American entry, and E. R. Thomas instructed his Buffalo factory to select a suitable car and prepare it. There were only four available, so selection was no great problem. Modifications were not extensive: the fenders were taken off and replaced by planks of rock elm 12 feet long by 2 inches thick, for use in mud and snow. An extra seat was mounted at the rear, storage lockers were rigged up, and the driver was provided with a heater: holes were drilled in the floor to admit engine heat!

The newspapers *Le Matin* of Paris and the New York *Times* sponsored the race, and the start was made, on February 12, 1908, from Times Square in New York, with 250,000 people watching. The weather was foul. The cars had barely left New York when they hit the worst blizzard in ten years, with three feet of snow banked in places. The Thomas was first in Chicago, thirteen days later. The Sizaire-Naudin had given up, the Motobloc and the De Dion were far behind, and only the Protos was a threat. That was to be the way of it, for the rest of the distance to Paris.

In Cheyenne on March 6, the Thomas lost its driver, Montague Roberts, who had a prior commitment to drive in a race on the East Coast in April. Linn Mathewson and Harold Brinker drove to San Francisco, and there George Schuster, originally signed on as mechanic, took over. From that point on the race was a tapestry of villainy, heroism, skulduggery, Homeric effort, two-timing and bribery. The Protos, three weeks behind in Utah, threw two connecting rods and its driver, Lieutenant Hans Koeppen, shipped it by rail 1000 miles to Seattle. He shipped the car to Vladivostok as well, bypassing Japan. Schuster drove to Seattle and drove across Japan. Protos cornered the gasoline supply in Vladivostok, and jumped the gun on the start. Nevertheless, when Schuster caught up with the Protos, to find it helplessly bogged down in mud, he put down his two planks and pulled it out. The Thomas broke its transmission running on the Trans-Siberian railway tracks and was sixteen days behind the Protos by the time it had been repaired. Still Schuster caught it again, fell behind again when a ferryboat sank under him. He was four days behind at Berlin and three days behind in Paris. But news of how the race had been run had preceded the cars; *Le Matin*'s correspondents had seen to that. Lieutenant Koeppen and the Protos were pointedly ignored; the celebration and the champagne waited for George Schuster and the Thomas.

SUCCESS

Year: *1907*
Model: *B*
Cylinders: *1*
Horsepower: *4*
Price: *$300*

The Success Automobile Buggy Manufacturing Company lived for three years, 1906–1909, in St. Louis, Missouri. The car was a good deal more buggy than automobile, even starker than most of its kind. It was really only a buggy with a motorcycle engine hung on it, a top speed around 10 miles an hour. It cost $275 with solid-steel tires. For an extra $25 the customer could specify hard rubber tires, but the Success designers would have nothing to do with pneumatics: ". . . with pneumatic tires, fully one-half of the power of the engine is absorbed in their Working and being 'Dragged' along the road." One rear wheel of the Success was driven, the other had the only brake on the vehicle. Steering was by chain, which very frequently fell off. Fortunately, the vehicle couldn't go fast enough fully to exploit its potential for trouble.

STEARNS

Year: *1908*
Model: *45/90*
Cylinders: *6*
Horsepower: *90*
Price: *$6250*

Frank B. Stearns made this car, rather less than midway in his career, which ran from 1899 to 1919—although he had made a car in 1896, three years before he established a factory in Cleveland. It was called a "Light Touring Car," but this Stearns had a monster of an engine, 800 cubic inches, and everything ran on ball bearings. Few six-cylinder Stearns cars were made, and those on special order only. It was considered the fastest stock car of its time, and Barney Oldfield won one of the early Mount Wilson hillclimbs with it. Al Poole won the Bright Beach 24-hour race with a Stearns in 1910, doing 1253 miles at an average of 52 MPH. The Stearns was severely tested before delivery, each chassis, before being bodied, doing 150 miles over very rough road under a load of half-a-ton of sand. When the body did go on it was given seventeen coats of paint.

The company was finally taken over by Willys after Stearns's departure, became Stearns-Knight and left

the scene in 1929.

WELCH

Year: *1909*
Model: *4–0*
Cylinders: *4*
Horsepower: *50*
Price: *$4700*

The use of double overhead camshafts operating valves in a hemispherical combustion chamber is an identifier of the modern high-performance engine and has been since Ernest Henry designed the 1912 racing Peugeot around it, but the little-known Welch, made in Pontiac, Michigan, from 1904 to 1911, quietly anticipated the idea, wildly radical at the time, although with only one camshaft. The telescopic steering column, thought brightly original when it was offered on sports cars in the late 1940's, was a feature of some Welch cars. The transmission was unusual, selection of each of the three forward speeds being arranged by lever-actuated clutch, with a separate lever for reverse.

This Welch Close-Coupled Touring car will do 60 miles an hour or so, and, like most machines of the period, covers ground with a comfortable if rather rocking, rolling sort of gait. It carries a notable expression of the class-consciousness of the period in a quasi–rumble seat hung on the rear of the body. This accommodation, the catalogue stated, was "for the man who wishes to sometimes drive [sic] his own car but take his chauffeur along without giving him the best seat in the car (beside the driver) or putting him in with his family." Next to being strapped underneath the vehicle next to the driveshaft, like an old-time hobo riding the rods, it's hard to see where a man could be put with more assurance of total discomfort. Bouncing along with nothing to look at but the back of the tonneau, or the cartwheel hats of the ladies in the rear seat, the luckless chauffeur rode in a low-pressure area, a moving fog of exhaust fumes, dust, road tar and chicken feathers, no doubt in perpetual terror as he contemplated the ineptitude of the amateur at the throttle. Mercifully, he would be the last to know about the accident—and probably the last to recover from it, too.

E.M.F.

Year: *1909*
Model: *30*
Cylinders: *4*
Horsepower: *30*
Price: *$1250*

Named after the Messrs. B. F. Everitt, William Metzger and Walter Flanders, the E.M.F. was a good automobile with little that was radical about it except perhaps the location of its transmission on the rear axle, not a common practice in 1909. Its dead-straight front axle and Mercer-like radiator made a pleasing composition. There were two body types available: a five-passenger touring car, or a four-passenger "Tourabout," an E.M.F. innovation: a rumble seat was supplied, without extra charge, to be interchanged with the car's regular rear seat. The E.M.F. was a sturdy automobile—the 1909 Glidden Tour Committee used an E.M.F. as a pathfinder car—and it was popular in the Middle West as a farmer's car. A business fight with Studebaker, which eventually absorbed it, made the company short-lived. Studebaker used the E.M.F. name until 1913. The use of initials in a name was risky in the infancy of the automobile, and E.M.F. was variously rendered as "Every morning fix-em," "Every man's folly," "Every mechanical fault," "Eternally missing fire," and "Every mechanic's friend."

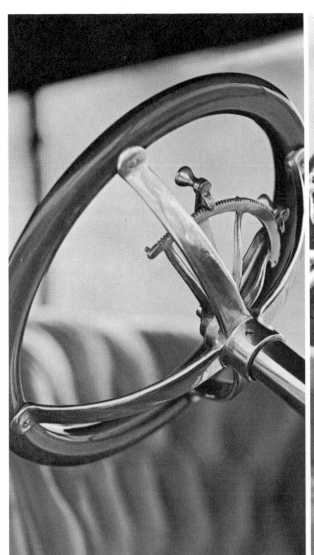

STANLEY

Year: *1909*
Model: *E2*
Cylinders: *2*
Horsepower: *10*
Price: *$850 (+$25 for rumble seat)*

Francis E. and Freelan O. Stanley were Maine boys, and Yankees to the bone. They were identical twins and enjoyed defying identification: only close friends and associates could tell them apart, and they liked posing for photographs that showed their profiles, alike as the Indians on a couple of buffalo nickels, side by side. They had a taste for practical jokes. It was said of them that they would go out in identical cars, one a couple of miles ahead, for a bit of police-baiting. If Mr. F. E., in the lead car, was stopped, the policeman would shortly be startled by the sight of Mr. F. O. whistling past in what looked to be the same automobile. They were rich men before they got around to the automobile business. They had turned an honest dollar in oddly assorted ways: they produced the first successful factory-made violins in the United States; they developed early Roentgen (X-ray) equipment, built illuminating-gas generators and were pioneers in the photographic dry-plate field. (Pioneer photographers like the great Mathew Brady had to prepare their own wet plates and use them immediately.)

In 1896, when they were forty-seven, the Stanleys saw a steam-driven horseless carriage at a county fair. The thing was badly designed and poorly built, and the twins (most stories hold that Mr. F. E. had the idea first) decided to show the world how it should be done. The first Stanley ran in October 1897, and ran well. A year later, they put on a show at a short track in Cambridge, Massachusetts. They ran a mile at an average of 27, and two miles at 22 MPH and had to fight off eager customers. One year more and they were in business: they had sold 200 cars. One of their earliest customers, Lorenzo Barber, formed a partnership with J. B. Walker to form the Locomobile Company, and this corporation bought out the Stanleys, lock, stock and barrel, for $250,000, on condition they make no steam cars for two years. They also sold out their dry-plate photographic business, to Eastman Kodak, for another fortune. They had nothing to do, so they decided to make more steam automobiles. They spent a year redesigning the car, so as not to infringe the patents they had sold to Locomobile. There was some fuss, but the Locomobile contract ran out in May 1901 anyway; Barber and Walker had split up, and the Stanleys were able to buy back their original patents for very little. They began the second phase of their production in May of 1902 and were soon running merrily at a production rate of a thousand a year or so. Their racing successes were splendid; one of them, Fred Marriott's 127.6 MPH at Ormond Beach, Florida, was a world record and the first time any man had reached two miles a minute in any vehicle. Next year, Marriott hit a small bump on the beach at what he believed was a much higher velocity and became airborne for 100 feet or so; the car was demolished and Marriott very seriously injured. In a typically forthright decision, Mr. F. E. and Mr. F. O. announced that the factory would never race again. All their decisions were like that. They had no stockholders, no board of directors, nobody to consult except each other, which they seemed to do most usually in the mornings, sitting on the steps of the plant, whittling and conversing elliptically. They habitually came to work just as the night watchman was leaving. They wouldn't advertise, sell on credit, or give a guarantee, maintaining that to be asked for a guarantee was to be insulted—if anything went wrong through fault of theirs, they'd fix it, without question.

The Stanleys retired in 1917 and Mr. F. E. was killed the next year in one of his own cars. Running fast along a country road near Ipswich, Massachusetts, he came around a corner to find two farmers, wagon-mounted, having a chat. It wasn't a hard decision to make: into the wagons or off the road, and Mr. F. E. went off the road. Mr. F. O. lived until 1940, when he died of a heart attack, nine years short of his hundredth year. The last car bearing the Stanley name had been made in 1925.

THOMAS

Year: *1909*
Model: *L6–40*
Cylinders: *6*
Horsepower: *40*
Price: *$3000*

This lithe and lovely red touring car is a direct descendant of the Thomas Flyer that won the 1908 New York-to-Paris race (pages 44–45). It is called a Flyabout. The body is hand-formed aluminum, which makes the car far lighter than it looks, at 2500 pounds, and it would do 70 miles an hour.

BRUSH

Year: *1910*
Model: *D–24*
Cylinders: *1*
Horsepower: *10*
Price: *$500*

The price of a good horse and buggy, Alanson P. Brush announced in 1911, was enough to buy one of his runabouts. The figure he had in mind was $485. The chassis *and* the axles were made of wood—oak, hickory or rock maple, air-dried and oil-soaked—and suspension was by the then revolutionary system of coil springs, although they were under tension, not compression, as was nearly always afterward the custom. The wooden axles were said to contribute to riding comfort, being somewhat more flexible and resilient than steel. Another oddity was that the one-cylinder engine ran counterclockwise. (This put off some prospective buyers, who were nervous enough about cranking without having to remember to do it the wrong way around. Left-handers liked it, though.) "Everyman's car," the Brush was called, "not a big, high-powered, high-priced car." The businessman was urged to consider that he could get to his office "quicker than by street-car, cheaper than by train, and the fresh morning air will fit you for the day's work." (The standard Runabout model had no windshield.) The Brush was one of the first cars to use left-hand steering. Benjamin Briscoe bought up Brush Runabout as part of the big combine, United States Motors, which he set up in 1910.

Alanson Brush had another card in his hand: he had designed the Oakland—*its* engine ran "backward," too—and the Oakland became the Pontiac, so that Brush is still, in a tenuous way, represented in the industry today. The Oakland, "The Car With a Conscience," was first to be finished in Charles F. Kettering's revolutionary Duco, a fast-drying finish that tremendously speeded up the production lines of 1924, the year it came in. Before the Duco process, coach-painting was the normal thing, the laying on, by brush or spray—brush, if it was to be really a quality job—of many coats of ground color, laboriously hand-rubbed with felt blocks and rottenstone and cold water, finished with two or three coats of the finest pale varnish for sheen.

ROLLS-ROYCE

Year: *1910*
Model: *Silver Ghost*
Cylinders: *6*
Horsepower: *48*
Price: *$7500 (chassis)*

The incomparable reputation of the Rolls-Royce automobile was founded on this car, the model first called by the factory the 40/50. The company had been founded, in 1904, on the meeting of Henry Royce, master mechanic, and the Hon. Charles S. Rolls, third son of Baron Llangattock, sportsman, motorist, aviator, and dealer in French and Belgian automobiles. Royce built his first car because he was appalled at the roughness and noise of a Decauville he had bought for his own use; and Rolls was attracted to him because the third Royce car came to his attention and made his own importations appear to be so crude. Rolls's function was to put up capital and to sell the vehicle; Royce was to make it. By the time Rolls was killed in an aircraft accident in 1910 the firm was irresistibly on the road to business immortality.

The "Silver Ghost" (the name was given it by the legendary Claude Johnson, next to Royce himself the most important executive in the company) was in essential design a very ordinary motorcar. There was nothing radical about Royce, and there was nothing radical about his car. (He arrived at the bore and stroke dimensions by striking an average among contemporary engines!) What *was* radical about Royce was his methodology; it was radical, but very simple: buy the best material available; put it together in the

best possible fashion; test every single part you make until it breaks, and then do it better, so that it will *not* break.

Royce considered himself first and foremost a master mechanic. Even after he had been knighted he signed himself in a guestbook "Henry Royce, Mechanic." He had been brought up in the hard school of Victorian hand craftsmanship. When he was an apprentice in the Great Northern Railway shops a man wasn't thought to have approached competence until he could file a square on a round brass rod by hand and eye so that it would fit a square hole filed in a brass sheet, without a sliver of light showing through. Cars made to that kind of standard were superior to the ordinary product of the time on such a scale that there was almost no comparison. As one of fifty examples that might be cited, Rolls-Royce chassis were not riveted together when the Silver Ghost was made (they are now). They were put together by *tapered* bolts press-fitted into hand-reamed holes. The result was an automobile that would, if decently maintained, run nicely for 500,000 miles.

The Silver Ghost was in continuous production from 1906 to 1925, the longest continuous run of any model in history. This particular touring car came from the famous Sword collection in Scotland.

58

DURYEA

Year: *1910*
Model: *Not designated*
Cylinders: *2*
Horsepower: *12/15*
Price: *$675*

In a paper he wrote as a schoolboy, Charles Duryea predicted, "The humming of flying machines will be music over all lands, and Europe will be distant but a half day's journey." The Duryea brothers—Charles Edgar and J. Frank Duryea—were mechanically gifted, and their claim to have run—in Springfield, Massachusetts, in September 1893—the first true gasoline automobile made in the United States is a strong one. Unhappily, the brothers quarreled, and the division grew into one of the bitterest family schisms in industrial history. In later years, Charles Duryea tended to use the first person singular in talking about the Duryea car, as, "It is my belief that I designed and built the first gasoline automobile actually to run in America, sold the first car on this side, did the first automobile advertising and won the first two American races. The last two claims cannot be disputed; the first two have been, though no one else offers proofs acceptable in court, as I do, of operation of a gasoline vehicle as early as April 19, 1892, or sales as early as the summer of 1896." J. Frank Duryea, on the other hand, more often said "we" than "I" as consistent with his contention that his brother had designed the car but that he had largely built it. He said little in public, however, until 1937, when he said in print that most of his brother Charles's ideas for the car had proven unworkable, and that Charles had neither seen nor ridden in the first Duryea. The issue is now extremely complicated and the documentation on it monumental. A minor example of statements that can start furious arguments among Duryea partisans: the Smithsonian Institution, in 1948, changed its credit from Charles alone to Charles and Frank; the *World Almanac*, in 1949, did the same. On the other hand, the patent for the car, filed on April 30, 1894, was in Charles's name alone.

The brothers parted company professionally in 1898. J. Frank designed the Stevens-Duryea, of which about ten thousand units were sold. Charles was connected with various automobile companies. This very rare Buggyaut, one of his interests, was not a success, being quite out-of-date in design by the time it appeared.

MERCER

Year: *1910*
Model: *C*
Cylinders: *4*
Horsepower: *34*
Price: *$1950*

This is the oldest known Mercer, called a Speedster, ancestor of the Raceabout on pages 72–73. The Mercer company was formed in 1909 and began production in 1910. The engine was by the Beaver Manufacturing Company of Milwaukee. A Mercer-designed engine was offered in 1911. The color is a yellow peculiar to the make. This Mercer is unique, as far as is known, and therefore irreplaceable, among the most valuable antique automobiles in the world.

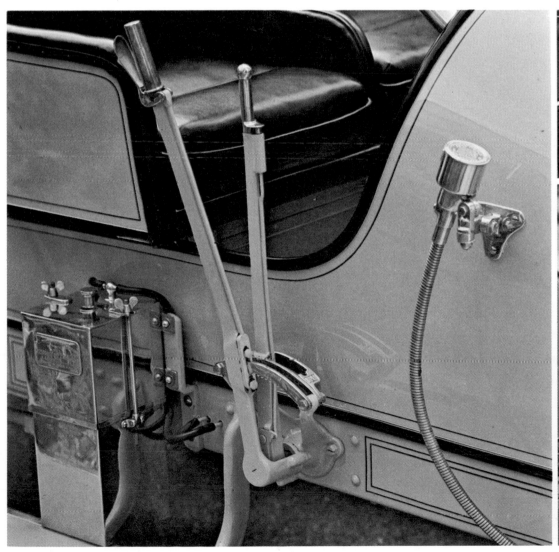

INTERNATIONAL

Year: *1912*
Model: *MW*
Cylinders: *2*
Horsepower: *20*
Price: *$950*

The "W" in this International model designation signifies water-cooling; most of the International Harvester Company's early output was cooled by air, each of the two finned cylinders having its own small fan. An ingenious automatic oiling system was built in, and there were two forward speeds and reverse. International clung stubbornly to the horse-and-wagon look, naturally enough, since the reputation of the firm had been made in horse-drawn farm equipment. But the huge wood-spoked wheels, buggy-seats, full-elliptic carriage springing, even the front dashboards, on the earliest models, were all anachronistic. The International was a useful device, though. The rear seat could be removed on most models, to allow it to carry light goods and serve as a delivery van. This Harrah car, for example, has a cargo space measuring 67 by 35 inches. The International Auto-Wagon and Auto-Buggy laid the seed for today's International trucks.

COEY FLYER

Year: *1913*
Model: *A*
Cylinders: *6*
Horsepower: *50*
Price: *$2000*

This magnificent white-and-gold car, a four-passenger touring barouche in the grand manner, was built in Chicago. The Coey company lived through a short span of time, 1911–1914. A feature of the car, not visible here, was a generous clearance between the top and the windshield, a whimsy guaranteed to provide the back-seat riders with ample ventilation. The tires are three feet in diameter by four inches, and the speedometer is mounted in rather a dashing fashion out of doors, and directly under the driver's eye. C. A. Coey, who designed this car, and the Coey Junior which succeeded it, was an early associate with the Thomas Company, and is said to have coined the name "Flyer" in connection with that car. He was a gentleman of parts: a race driver, proprietor of an early school of motoring, a man quick with his fists. A Coey car of any description is a rarity, and this is probably the best example of the make in existence.

CADILLAC

Year: *1913*
Model: *1913*
Cylinders: *4*
Horsepower: *40/50*
Price: *$1975*

The V–8 engine, today thought to be as modern as the minute, is really quite an old device, at least as old as 1907, and in 1916, indeed, there were twenty-three V–8's on the American market. But very probably the best of them was the Cadillac, a milestone-triumph in the life of Henry M. Leland, better-known still for the Lincoln. Leland was sixty-two when he went to Cadillac in 1904, and he created there a revolution: he insisted upon, enforced, indeed almost created the idea of absolute interchangeability of parts. Before Leland, the master mechanic was king. He hand-fitted, scraped, filed, modified and assembled every engine, and no two were quite alike. Leland changed all that, and proved that he had changed it with the winning of the DeWar Trophy in 1908. He—or Cadillac, which was to say the same thing—won it again, with the 1912 electric self-starter and the electrical system that went with it. The *idea* of the electric starter was not Leland's, nor was it Charles F. Kettering's. Ferdinand Porsche catalogued a self-starter as an option before Cadillac, and a dozen systems other than electric had been tried: compressed air, springs, acetylene gas, and whatnot. But Leland decided that the electric motor was the answer, and Kettering, using a cash register, of all things, as a springboard, decided that a 6-volt motor could be made to produce a momentary surge of power at 24 volts, enough to swing a cold engine, and the thing was done. One no longer had to be a shot-putter to start a car. Women could do it, and the Automobile Age was born.

From that day to this, Cadillac has been a standard of the world. Leland left the firm in 1917, after having operated under *carte blanche* from the irascible William Durant, who told him at the beginning, when Cadillac was absorbed by General Motors: "Run the company as if it were your own; no one will interfere with you." Cadillac offered the first high-speed V–8, brought the silent timing chain from Europe, and enforced the highest standards of quality control and inspection. The Cadillac V–16, Fisher-bodied, was the epitome of luxury; a 1966 Cadillac asks no quarter of anything made in the world today. And in the 1950's, Cadillac engines powered the big rumbling Allards that dominated U.S. sports-car racing.

FORD

Year: *1913*
Model: *T*
Cylinders: *4*
Horsepower: *20*
Price: *$525*

Little that everyone doesn't know can be said about Henry Ford, and it would be difficult indeed to exaggerate his stature. He was a mover and a shaker. Life when he left it was not what it had been when he found it. He changed the world, he touched the existence of hundreds of millions of people. He found the automobile a luxury, almost a rich man's toy; he left it a necessity.

Henry Ford was born during the Civil War—in 1863—and made his first automobile in 1896. By 1899 he had built a better one. He joined the Detroit Automobile Company, which failed. The quickest and cheapest path to fame in the automobile business, then as now, was racing, and Ford began to build race cars. He made good ones. He hired Barney Oldfield as a driver, and he drove himself, as well. Indeed, for a time he was a world record-holder: a mile in 39.1 seconds in 1904, on the famous "999" car. His earlier racing successes brought money, and he set up his company in 1903. His first cars were small and light, and fairly successful, excluding the big Model K, which was his partners' idea, not Ford's. He sold a good many of his Models N and S and R, and then in 1908 he turned out the Model T.

The Ford Model T was as close to an expression of genius as any automobile has been, indeed one might say, as close as any mechanical device has been. It expressed, with almost absolute purity, Ford's idea that the automobile should be a universal tool. To be a universal tool, it had to be *practical*, and practical the Model T certainly was. It was a miracle of design for its time, utterly simple, so simple that any bright blacksmith could maintain it, and while it was cheap, it was made of the best procurable materials. A Model T was a *lasting* car. And it was easy to drive. It didn't even have a gearshift lever requiring delicate coordination with a clutch. The transmission was planetary and pedal-operated. To get under way, you held the left-hand pedal down until the thing was moving well in first gear, then let it up, for high, and that was it. Reverse had a pedal of its own. (In moments of extreme stress, you could use reverse as a brake!) Maintenance was nothing. For example, the engine, clutch, transmission and driveshaft universals were all lubricated by engine oil. You could buy parts anywhere. It was the farmer's delight. It should have been: it rode so high that rutted roads bothered it little, it would climb the side of a house, if not forward, then backward, it would turn very nearly in its length, and when Ford was asked how much room there should be on the floor in front of the rear seats, he said, "Room enough for a milk-can." Ford kept cutting the price from the original $850 until, in 1924, he'd brought it down to $290! He made 15,456,868 Model T's from 1908 to 1927.

A truly successful automobile inevitably attracts accessory-makers, and hundreds of men made comfortable livings supplying oddments for the Model T, everything from instruments and lights to complete bodies. "Speedster" bodies like this one could be bought, or they could be run up at home. You could stick anything on a Model T. They were everything, ambulances, delivery trucks, police wagons, popcorn carts, zoo-keeper's trucks. There is something of the Model T Ford in every motorcar that has been built since 1910. It was the Universal Automobile.

MERCER

Year: *1913*
Model: *Series J. Type 35*
Cylinders: *4*
Horsepower: *58*
Price: *$2600*

It's likely that no one of the five-thousand-odd makes of automobile we have seen has so appreciated in value as the Mercer Raceabout of 1911–1914. Priced new at about $2600, it is worth today between $15,000 and $20,000. There are fewer than thirty extant, but this circumstance is not enough to account for the inflation. There are only six Bugatti Royales in the world, and they haven't increased in value eight times. (It would be interesting if they had: one Royale is definitely known to have cost $43,000 in 1931; on the Mercer scale, it would be worth $344,000 today.)

The 1911–1914 Mercer Raceabout, usually called the T-head, after the configuration of its engine, was an extraordinarily happy design. Despite its starkness, it's esthetically very pleasing, as any truly functional device is pleasing. It was fast, guaranteed by the factory to do 75 miles an hour, and by the standards then obtaining, extraordinarily roadable. It was esteemed in its day, and the designer, a delightful gentleman named Finlay Robertson Porter, lived to see the product of his tenure as chief engineer of the Mercer Company become the most sought-after of American-made cars. He died in 1964, aged ninety-two.

The Mercer's all-out-of-doors driving position gave one a remarkable sense of control, and it is a delight to take one over a mildly winding road on a warm day. (There are notable disadvantages to driving a Mercer in cold weather, not the least of them being the position of the accelerator, just over a brass stirrup *outside* the body; the wind has a tendency to funnel up one's trouser-leg.) The steering, terribly heavy at low speeds in the manner of the time, is pleasant and quick when the car is moving fast; the engine has a great deal of torque at low revolutions-per-minute, so that one can set the car at a hill in fourth gear and go up, as the expression used to be, with the engine "firing once to the telephone pole." The brakes are next to useless, but this rather lends spice to the proceedings, requiring one to plan a long way ahead. In its day one could buy a Mercer off the showroom floor, take it to a race course and run with good hope of winning.

AMERICAN

Year: *1914*
Model: *644*
Cylinders: *6*
Horsepower: *70*
Price: *$2750*

"A Car for the Discriminating Few" was one of the tag-lines used to sell the American Underslung. Another made reference to its comparative quietness of operation: "No Noise but the Wind." That, incidentally, could have been of considerable decibel value, because the exposed lamps, hood-straps, folding-irons and general gimcrackery on some early touring cars set up a remarkable racket even at moderate speeds, and a big car like the American might run up to 70 miles an hour.

The Underslung was one of the first creations of the great Harry C. Stutz. He had made a powered buggy-like vehicle when he was barely out of his twenties, he had worked for the Marion Company and sold Schebler carburetors, and his design for American clearly showed his original bent. The frame rode below the axles, not over, or on them, as was universal practice. This gave a low center of gravity—although the road clearance was high, at 11 inches—and allowed a dead-straight driveshaft from engine to differential, without the interposition of the usual universal joints to change the direction of the thing. Some Underslungs had wheels big enough to require 41-inch tires. On this Harrah car, they are 38 x 4½. The big wheels were indeed an advantage on the roads of the day, since they would not drop into every little pothole that came along. There was a certain amount of give in their long and slender wooden spokes, too. This was an idea that attracted engineers of the time. One attempted solution was that of the Ingram-Hatch Corporation, a short-lived enterprise of Staten Island, New York. Ingram-Hatch wheels were spoked in spring steel, with compressed-air cushions set between the spokes for further absorption of road shock. The wheels were shod in steel-and-leather tires. The Norwalk car, a West Virginia effort, was another that carried the frame beneath the axles in the underslung mode. The term survives no longer—except in the journalistic abomination "low-slung," almost automatically applied to any sports or imported automobile.

HUPMOBILE

Year: *1914*
Model: *32*
Cylinders: *4*
Horsepower: *32*
Price: *$1300*

The Hupmobile was one of the dozens of cars named by adding "mobile" to something, in this case the name of the designer, Robert C. Hupp. (Sometimes a characteristic of the car was indicated, as in the Frontmobile, an early front-wheel-drive model. The first Ford announcements called it a "Fordmobile.")

The firm was founded in 1908 and Hupp left three years later to make something called the R.C.H., being contractually forbidden to use his own name. (Another example of the same procedure was R. E. Olds's departure from Oldsmobile to make the Reo.)

Hupmobile went on for a long time, until 1941. The early cars, particularly the small runabouts, were well worth what they cost, which was little: $750 for the 1909 four-cylinder open model, for example. Hupmobiles ran in a few competitions, too, although they were not prominent in any really big-league events. Some of them were interesting, however, like the Flag-to-Flag Contest of 1910, a run from Denver, Colorado, to Mexico City, as it was called then. Hupmobile acquired the Chandler and Cleveland interests in 1928.

IMP

Year: *1914*
Model: *Not designated*
Cylinders: *2*
Horsepower: *10/15*
Price: *$375*

The Imp Cyclecar was made in Auburn, Indiana, and not for long—1913 and 1914. It was one of the best of a breed that never found a niche for itself.

The idea behind the cyclecar is clear in its name: build a vehicle that will be more comfortable than a motorcycle and cheaper than a car. It seemed an excellent notion, indeed foolproof and as sure of success as the steamboat, but only two cyclecars really gained acceptance, the British G.N. and the Morgan.

Most cyclecars had a wooden frame, as the Imp did, and drive by chain or belt or, sometimes, manila rope. Big single or two-cylinder engines were the rule. The Imp's was air-cooled and had a fan to help the process along. The exhaust arrangements were novel: the pipes ran forward instead of backward, emptying into two large mufflers mounted vertically beside the front wheels. The steering post ran down the dead center of the car between the two cylinders of the V–2 engine. The driver and his single passenger rode tandem, the passenger in the rear, not, oddly, a universally favored arrangement. At least one cyclecar was set up to be steered from the back seat, with the passenger in front, next to the accident, and quite incapable of doing anything about it. What appeared to be yards of leather belting carried the power from the front-mounted engine to the rear wheels.

The Morgan Three-Wheeler (pages 186–187) is not usually thought of as a cyclecar although it was one in all but the strictest definition; it didn't have four wheels. The G.N. was a cyclecar named after its designers, H. R. Godfrey and Archie Frazer-Nash (Godfrey later made the H.R.G.—Halford-Robbins-Godfrey—and Frazer-Nash the Frazer-Nash, best known of all chain-driven automobiles).

The Imp had a proper rod-and-ball-joint steering system, but such niceties were uncommon on cyclecars, and the G.N. used a wire-and-bobbin system, which is one step up from rope-steering a Flexible Flyer. But the G.N. was light, and so fast for its class that it made a formidable sprint and hillclimb car. Its competition successes were probably responsible for keeping it in vogue until the end of the cyclecar era, around 1914.

BRISCOE

Year: *1915*
Model: *B-15*
Cylinders: *4*
Horsepower: *24*
Price: *$785*

When Benjamin Briscoe's United States Motor Company failed in 1912, he and a couple of his engineers went to France to study design. It was a sensible, even a wise idea, because France, which had been the cradle of the automobile, was still a long way from the decadence that began in the late 1930's and which has left her today with only four of the great names: Citroën, Peugeot, Panhard, Renault. In the years before the First World War there were uncounted numbers of French makes in existence. Some of them, like the Berger or the Reyrol, are known only to archivists; but France had its full share of giants like the three first named above, and Bugatti, Voisin, De Dion—not to mention some wonderful eccentrics.

Briscoe claimed to have been duly inspired, and by 1915, reorganized and back in business, he was offering what he called "The First French Car at an American Price." It had been, he said, designed to his commission by a Paris house and represented the latest in Continental advancement. The single headlamp was not a common French design point, but it did put the Briscoe past confusion with any other make. The light was not merely hung on the front of the car, it was faired into the radiator shell. In order to spare oncoming nighttime motorists the illusion that they were about to pass a motorcycle, extra-large cowl lamps were fitted to the Briscoe.

When the car first entered the market it was priced at $750, but for that money the purchaser did indeed get a basic motorcar: it had no top, windshield, speedometer, starter or generator. These were optional at a total extra cost of $900. Later on Briscoe was able to offer a complete package for the price cited for this "cloverleaf" roadster.

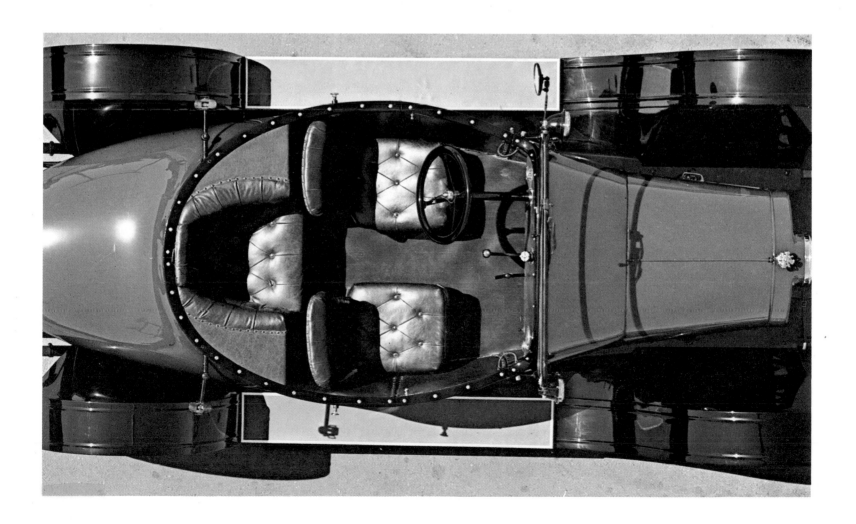

FIAT

Year: *1915*
Model: *Type 35 TER*
Cylinders: *4*
Horsepower: *25/35*
Price: *$3600*

Giovanni Agnelli set up the company Società Italiana per la Costruzione e il Commercio delle Automobili Torino in 1899; but someone, perhaps the man in charge of laying out the firm's letterhead, prevailed upon Agnelli to change the name to Fabbrica Italiana Automobili Torino, and Agnelli's associate Aristide Faccioli suggested using the firm's initials as the car name: F.I.A.T. The name ran that way until 1906 when it was changed into the word Fiat, still used today by the company that produces an overwhelming percentage of all the wheeled vehicles made in Italy.

Monster-engined F.I.A.T. cars did well in early racing, and no account of the 1905 running of the Vanderbilt Cup on Long Island is complete without mention of Vincenzo Lancia's draining a pint of champagne just before the start of the race, and of his leading the first 100 miles of the race in his 110-horsepower F.I.A.T. (A collision with Walter Christie put him out for an hour, and he finished fourth. Later on he started his own factory, also still in existence and still making fine motorcars.)

This Fiat roadster came from Poughkeepsie, not Turin. As Rolls-Royce was to do in the 1920's, Fiat set up a factory to produce for the American trade in 1915, not a long-lived project.

THE MAJESTIC

PIERCE-ARROW

Year: *1915*
Model: *48-B-3*
Cylinders: *6*
Horsepower: *48*
Price: *$6000*

All generalizations are false, including this one, the ancient Gallic cliché goes, but still it does seem a safe bet that the only birdcage manufacturer ever to enter the motorcar business was George N. Pierce of Buffalo, New York. Pierce made, if contemporary accounts are to be trusted, superior birdcages, and he certainly did make superior motorcars. He began, in 1901, by offering to the public a device called the Motorette, powered by a 2¾-horsepower proprietary engine—a De Dion. In five months he sold twenty-five of them, a respectable haul for the day. In 1903 he brought out the Arrow, a two-cylinder, 15-horsepower vehicle, and the Pierce-Stanhope. A year later the Great Arrow appeared, a 28-horsepower monster of forbidding mien. In 1905 a Great Arrow ran the Glidden Tour, 860 miles that year, with George N.'s son, Percy, at the helm, his parents and his fiancée riding passenger. The route was New York, Hartford, Boston, Portsmouth, Bretton Woods and return. The Great Arrow made the run with a loss of exactly four points out of the one thousand with which each contestant started— and fifteen of the other twenty-two drivers voted it the outstanding car of the Tour. In those faroff times in the United States, as in Europe now, a victory in a major race or rally was invaluable as sales ammunition, and the Buffalo factory prospered accordingly. Three years later the car was called the Pierce Great Arrow and in 1909 the "Great" was dropped. The Pierce-Arrow was launched as one of the fine luxury motor-carriages of the era. Prices ran from $5900 to $7200—for an equivalent figure today, multiply by at least 2.5. The factory exerted itself to make the car worth the money. The Rolls-Royce quality-control and inspection systems were emulated. Every component in every engine was inspected after every operation. The completed engine was run on a dynamometer, torn down, reinspected and reassembled. Another dynamometer test was run and it was dropped into a chassis. The entire rig was now put on a dynamometer, and, if it passed, a box seat was bolted on and the car test-driven. If it passed this test, the body was dropped on and the car taken to the road, not by a test-driver, but by an engineer. If the unit passed *that* test, it was sold. The customer received a car like this one, solid, quiet, completely equipped—umbrella-holder, chauffeur-telephone—and was content.

DODGE BROTHERS

Year: *1915*
Model: *Not designated*
Cylinders: *4*
Horsepower: *30/35*
Price: *$785*

The Dodge Brothers, Horace Elsin and John Francis, made something more than, say, $150,000,000 before they died, both in the same year, 1920, both in their early fifties. They had come into Detroit from out in the country around 1885, machinists and inseparable. They were early associates of Henry Ford, and each put $10,000 into his spindling company, $3000 in cash and $7000 in goods and services, 50 shares of stock apiece. They built engines and gears for Ford. John Francis Dodge was a vice president of the Ford Motor Company, and the Dodge Brothers were rich men in 1914 when they brought out the first car of their own making: an L-head four-cylinder. Dodge automobiles were rugged, if, as some critics said, a little rough. But they were lasters, and they could take it: the 1914 Dodge touring car was the official staff car for the American Expeditionary Forces in World War I. The Dodges built their cars on a moving production line reminiscent of Ford's, and they had one of the first test tracks in Detroit, a short wooden oval and a steep hillclimb. The New York brokerage house of Dillon, Read acquired control of the company in 1925 and Chrysler took it over in 1928.

The Dodge brothers were genuine dyed-in-the-wool pioneer types, as far removed from today's typical computer-bred executives as can be. The Dodges were swingers, men who favored long drinks and short arguments.

CRANE-SIMPLEX

Year: *1916*
Model: *5*
Cylinders: *6*
Horsepower: *110*
Price: *$10,000*

There was for a time a minor vogue in American automobilism which held it desirable that motorcars should look like speedboats, and this Crane-Simplex, bodied by Holbrook for A. M. Baxter, took the trend about as far as was feasible, from cowl ventilators on the bonnet to the hubcap for the rear-mounted spare, cast in the shape of a propeller. The car belonged to a Connecticut painter and illustrator, Melbourne Brindle, and was a familiar exhibit at shows in the area.

The Simplex family tree is complicated, the first one, according to the eminent authority and collector Henry Austin Clark, Jr., the Mercedes Simplex designed by Wilhelm Maybach. Smith & Mabley of New York built the first American car to carry the name, and it was frankly derivative. It was made of the best materials on the world market, including such luxuries as Krupp chrome-nickel steel, and few proprietary items were included. Smith & Mabley even made their own nuts and bolts, and went outside only

for tires, wheels and electrics. Simplex race cars, their profiles stark in the standard three elements of the period, tank, seats and bonnet, were hardy runners in the hairy competitions of the early 1900's, and Clark owns one such carrying a really impressive amount of tankage aft of the bucket seats: 40 gallons of gasoline, 13 of oil.

Smith & Mabley failed in the panic of 1907 and the firm came into the hands of Herman Broesel. On his death, the company was taken over by Goodrich, Lockhart and Smith of New York, and the new organization, in 1914, bought the Crane Motor Car Company of Bayonne, New Jersey, headed by Henry M. Crane, a noted engine-designer who specialized in speedboat powerplants and had produced a limited line of excellent and expensive automobiles. The Crane-Simplex was one of the best grand-scale motorcars of the period and was still on the market in 1920. Termination date for the company was 1925.

McFARLAN

Year: *1917*
Model: *127X*
Cylinders: *6*
Horsepower: *90*
Price: *$3200*

Over a span of not quite two decades, 1910–1918, the McFarlan was built in Connersville, Indiana, a big, expensive, exclusive kind of automobile. The engine was a monster, 572.5 cubic inches, with a bore and stroke of 4½ by 6 inches. McFarlan offered the client a wide choice of bodywork, colors, appointments. One catalogue laid down that "A motor car such as the McFarlan must reflect the individuality of the owner in much the same manner as his clothes; must above all be comfortable and at the same time appropriate and suited to the use to which it is to be put."

This example is a seven-passenger touring car. The extra seats are stored in a cabinet built into the second cowl and are completely hidden behind flexible wooden blinds. Between them is a compartment fitted for two quart-size Thermos bottles.

An advertisement of the time shows Jack Dempsey, a McFarlan owner, in one of the company's giant limousines, great drum-type headlights, a bumper sticking out what looks to be four feet in front of the radiator. The car so outscales Dempsey that he looks curiously small, as if he were a fairly sturdy flyweight.

STANLEY

Year: *1918*
Model: *735*
Cylinders: *2*
Horsepower: *20*
Price: *$2700*

Steam as motive power for the automobile seems so crushingly logical that at first glance it's hard to understand how the internal combustion engine managed to win what looked to be, in the beginning, a barely even three-cornered fight among steam, gasoline and electricity. The virtues of the steam engine are impressive, and two of them are particularly to the point: because the steam engine works at low speeds and low pressures, it is long-lived, and because it develops its full power when it is barely moving, it does not require the services of flywheel, clutch, transmission gears and so on (not to mention an ignition system, still, today, the biggest cause of engine failure on the road). A steam engine can be hooked directly to the driving wheels. It doesn't sit idling in traffic jams, blowing out carcinogenic vapors; when the car stops, the engine stops. Steam automobiles were fast enough. A Stanley made an official record of 127.66 miles an hour in 1907, and was not fully extended in doing it.

Why aren't we running on steam today, then? Probably because while the steam engine was simple, running it was not. Early Stanley Steamers, best-known of probably one hundred makes that were made in America, had more than a dozen controls. Before the introduction of the condenser, which allowed used steam to be turned back to water and used again, steamers needed filling up every fifty miles or so. They took as long as thirty minutes to start. Before the self-starter, which came into the American market on the Cadillac in 1912, drivers didn't mind the delay so much, since everyone had a friend who'd broken his arm cranking his car, but after that . . . the steamers needed instant starting, simple controls, long range. All these things came with the Doble in 1923: it would move off from dead cold in 30 seconds, its controls were simpler than a gas car's, it would do 95 miles an hour in eerie silence, but it was too late. The fight was over.

For the brothers F. O. and F. E. Stanley, identical twins, it had been a good thing. They built fine cars from 1899 to 1917, sold them on their own terms—cash on the barrelhead, mostly—and made and split two fortunes on them.

RAUCH & LANG

Year: *1919*
Model: *B26*
Cylinders: (*Electric*)
Horsepower: *10¾ (max.)*
Price: *$3350*

For the first couple of decades of the twentieth century, the electric was a fair bet to run away with all the marbles if the steamer didn't. To many people it still seems illogical that the electric and the steamer didn't do better. After all, they had such good starts: the first automobile to do 60 miles an hour, a mile a minute, was an electric, and the first to do 120 was a steamer.

The electric was the great *Le Jamais Contente*, a torpedo-like device mounted on wheels and stuffed full of batteries. In the capable hands of the Belgian *pilote* Camille Jenatzy it was gradually worked up until on April 29, 1899, it did 65.8 miles an hour over a flying kilometer.

Almost any good electric of the dozens that were made in the United States would do 60 miles an hour —for a couple of blocks. If one wanted to do, say, 30 miles in the course of the day, however, it was advisable to run more decorously. In the final stages of development, electrics would do 75 miles at 25 miles an hour, a capacity entirely adequate for town use. They were dead quiet. Like the steamers, they started themselves, and unlike the steamers, they were simplicity itself to drive. Usually the controller was a twistable handle on the steering tiller. The wiring of the batteries to set up the combinations for varying power requirements was complicated, but the driver didn't need to worry about it. At night the car was plugged into a home charger, rather an expensive rig, and was ready to go again in the morning. In an emergency you might be able to get to a big-city charging station, and a kit was sold which would help an enterprising "juicer" driver steal a charge from a trolley line. It was inadvisable to do this while standing in a puddle, since the trolley lines carried 550 or 600 volts. The batteries in a sizable electric like this Rauch & Lang would weigh more than 1000 pounds, and they lasted about three years.

Pleasant as they were in many ways, the electrics were doomed once their instant starting and silent travel characteristics didn't loom so large vis-à-vis gasoline cars. Rauch & Lang gave up in 1928, and the last maker, Detroit Electric, ten years later.

BRIGGS & STRATTON

Year: *1920*
Model: *D*
Cylinders: *1*
Horsepower: *2*
Price: *$125*

Having four wheels, two seats, a steering wheel and an engine, this device must qualify as an automobile, and, that being the case, it is reasonable to think it may be the cheapest ever built. Technically it is a "buckboard," so called after the light horse-drawn wagon, and there were a number of them on the market in the 1920's. The buckboards were akin to the cyclecars, but considerably more primitive. For example, cyclecars had springing, or suspension, in some form, fitted between body and axles, but this Briggs & Stratton did not; it relied on the resiliency and bounce in the long oak or hickory slats that made the body-cum-frame-cum-chassis. The engine was a fifth wheel that had been designed to power bicycles; it was called a "motor-wheel" and was a complete power-package: engine, drive, cooling fan and gasoline tank all tucked together.

The buckboards were started by lifting the motor-wheel off the ground (it rode on a pivoted lever) and manually spinning it. When it was warm and running the driver returned to his command post in front, lowered it slowly by remote control, so to speak, accepted a certain amount of tire-slippage in lieu of a clutch, and was off. He could expect, if he were not a speed maniac, to get nearly 100 miles to the gallon of gasoline; he could do 25 miles an hour flat-out, wide-open and crouched over, and the brakes were adequate for the small amount of weight they had to handle. (And it was possible, if inadvisable, to drag one's feet on the ground.)

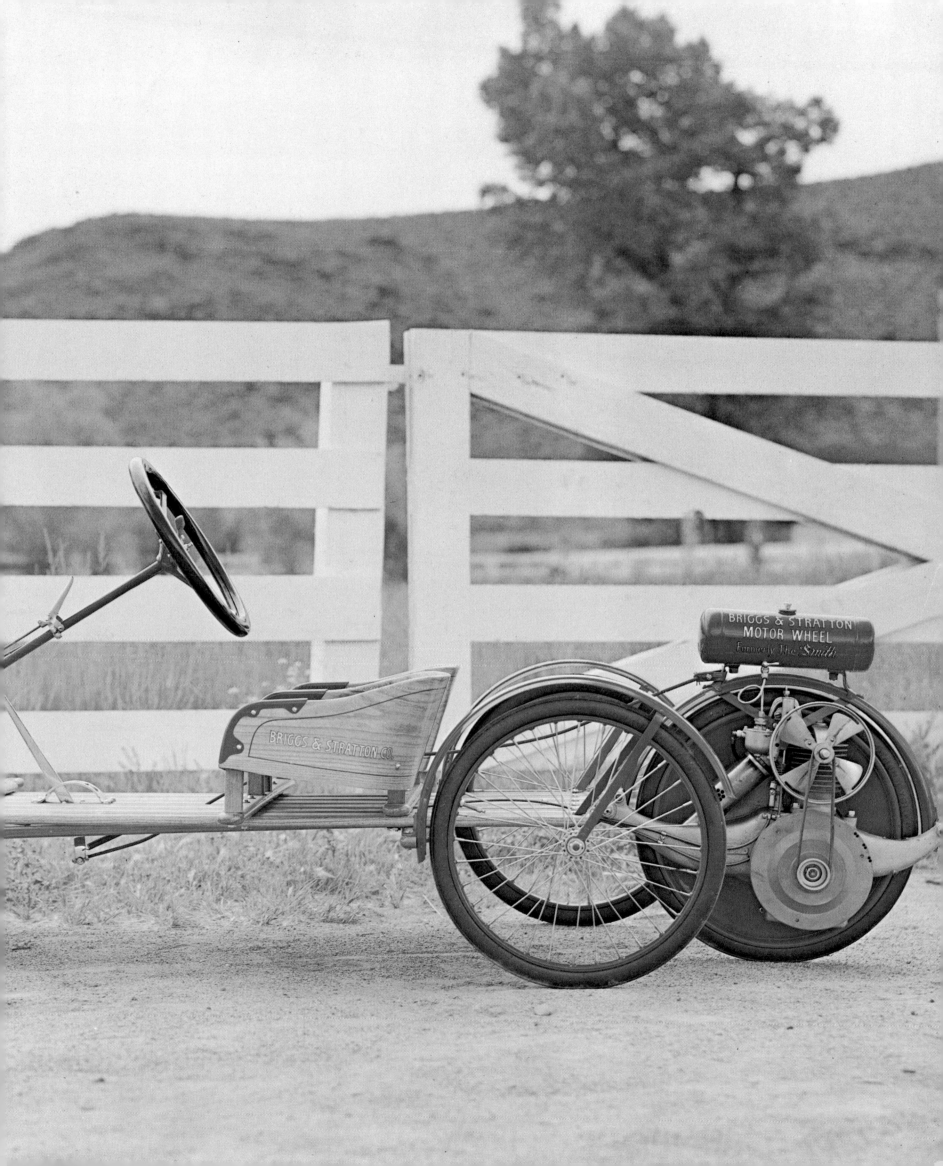

APPERSON

Year: *1920*
Model: *8.20*
Cylinders: *8*
Horsepower: *60*
Price: *$2950*

In any British pub, say in London or Birmingham for choice, where British motoring types congregate today, it's easy to get an argument on the startlingly different attitudes towards the automobile held by the Americans and the British. The matter soon comes down to a fine point: the Americans think of the automobile as they think of the television set or the radio or the oil-burner in the basement: a mechanical device, marvelous enough to be sure, designed to contribute significantly—and quietly—to creature comfort. The British view differs. The United Kingdom is still heavily populated with enthusiasts who view the automobile as an instrument of sport, a pleasure, a device through the mastery of which one can demonstrate one's skill, versatility, indeed even virility.

The first automobile I remember well was an Apperson Jack Rabbit. Its owner was our next-door neighbor. He was a machinist. He worked until noon on Saturdays, and by two o'clock he would be in his garage, working on his Jack Rabbit. Twice a year he stripped it to the last nut and bolt; weekly, he polished, rubbed, burnished, adjusted and cossetted the thing.

It seemed to me he rarely ran it, but when he did, it went soundlessly, it flowed, it fled along Owasco Street. He, Mr. Clark, was an Enthusiast—but this was 1923, 1924, or so. He has since gone to his reward, and his Apperson, I suppose, to the junkyard.

It was a splendid motorcar. Elmer and Edgar Apperson were pioneers of the first significance. They appear in the history books as associates of Elwood Haynes, in 1898. Indeed, engaged on a contract basis, they built the first Haynes car, and it ran in 1894. Time passed, and in 1902 the Appersons made a car of their own. It was a "raceabout" in the standard form of the day, an ancestor of the Mercer and the Stutz and the Simplex, a hooded engine, stalk-like steering post rising out of the slanted floorboard, bucket seats, cylindrical gasoline tank behind. In 1907, they offered the first of the Jack Rabbits. They were brilliant men, and innovators. For example, the first opposed-cylinder engine was of Apperson design. But they did not prosper wildly. Elmer died in 1920, Edgar sold out in 1922 and the last car to bear the name was made in 1925.

STUTZ

Year: *1920*
Model: *Series 4*
Cylinders: *4*
Horsepower: *80*
Price: *$3250*

This red roadster is the Stutz Bearcat famed in song and story as the wheeled symbol of the Flapper Era. It does not look a very dashing motorcar to us, rather heavy in front; but when it appeared in 1919 it was thought rakish, with its great steering wheel, the size of it made necessary by the leverage required to turn the front wheels, its flat-folding top, and the out-of-doors handbrake and gearshift levers. By 1920 most American manufacturers had decided that the driver should sit on the left, but the Bearcat was a lineal descendant of the 1911 Stutz race car, and in those pioneer days, race drivers rode on the right, their mechanics on the left.

The Bearcat was fast, immensely sturdy, and expensive. If one can believe some contemporary historians, the Ivy League colleges and the environs of upper Fifth Avenue and Michigan Boulevard swarmed with Bearcats in the hands of young blades invariably wearing raccoon coats, hip-flasked surely, and accompanied by at least one of the flat-chested, short-skirted, bobbed-hair ladies of the period. The Bearcat as a symbol of that period has come to be equated with Al Capone, the Charleston, bathtub gin, and a view of life stated as well as anyone by the ironmaster Charles Schwab: "Not only can everyone be rich, but everyone *ought* to be!"

All this is perhaps a bit out of phase. In my own passage through the twenties, granted I was but a youth in knickerbockers, I do not recall ever seeing a Stutz Bearcat, freighted with raccoon-coated wastrels or not, but then, I never saw Capone, either, or drank of bathtub gin. Indeed, the only evidence of the Dionysian revels of the decade that came before my eyes I saw in the pink dawn of a May day on the Cornell University campus, whence I had gone in my role as a humble delivery-boy of the Cornell *Sun*. The door of a fraternity house opened, and a girl of considerable beauty came out, wearing a fur coat, certainly not raccoon, slipped on the bottom step and fell flat on her back. She was wearing, under the coat, nothing. She arose with dignity and got into a car standing in the driveway. She started it and drove off, purposefully but on rather a serpentine course. It was not a Bearcat, it was a Packard.

HEINE-VELOX

Year: *1921*
Model: *C*
Cylinders: *12*
Horsepower: *75*
Price: *$17,000*

Forty-five hundred pounds of automobile built around a twelve-cylinder engine, the Heine-Velox is so rare an item that many collectors have never seen one. The car was made in San Francisco and the first model was held under test for a full year before being released. The extremely sloped windshield, designed with a low glare level in mind, was mounted in rubber, a long step forward for 1921. The brakes were rear-wheel mechanical. The instrument panel had a marked slope toward the horizontal, with the purpose of accessibility of minor controls and easy reading of the instruments. Instead of being laid on top of the chassis side-members, the body was dropped down around them, making a low appearance for the car overall, and somewhat lowering the center of gravity as well. The floor, entirely inside the frame, contributed usefully to the rigidity of the whole carriage. The trouble with the Heine-Velox was price: all bodies were custom, and the range was $17,000 to $25,000.

DORT

Year: *1922*
Model: *14C*
Cylinders: *4*
Horsepower: *35*
Price: *$1865*

The Dort was made in Flint, Michigan, during the decade 1915–1925. The company head, J. Dallas Dort, had been a partner of William Durant in the carriage-making business. The car was produced in no great quantity, and is a rarity today. The disc wheels on this three-passenger "Harvard Coupe" (there was a "Yale" as well) were thought very dashing and had the practical advantage of being easy to clean. Wire wheels were hard to get at, and wood-spoked wheels, the so-called "artillery" type, while good-looking in the classic sense, were subject to breakage and deterioration.

FORD

Year: *1922*
Model: *T*
Cylinders: *4*
Horsepower: *47*
Price: *$707*

This was an expensive Ford, priced at three times the chassis cost ($285), the difference going into high-performance equipment. For in addition to every other use the Model T was put to, it could be made into a racing car like this Ames-bodied example. The changes involved a Frontenac cylinder head, Pasco wire wheels, carburetor and intake manifold by Winfield. It would do 5–40 MPH in 16 seconds. Ordinary Ford steering was nearly as quick as a born race car's, and if the brakes were by no means up to the velocity it didn't really matter; track racing was the order of the day, and in track racing brakes weren't of paramount significance.

WILLS SAINTE CLAIRE

THE GREAT

Year: *1922*
Model: *A-68*
Cylinders: *8*
Horsepower: *65*
Price: *$2475*

Wills Sainte Claire was not long on the scene, from 1921 to 1926. It deserved a longer life, because it was a very fine motorcar. It was the creation of one of the few men who could say in verity that he had punched Henry Ford on the jaw, one Childe Harold Wills. He did not strike the great Ford in anger, however, but in sport. Wills and Ford worked together as draftsmen long before the Model T came down the line, and they used to box for amusement—and to keep warm in the cold office they shared. Childe Harold Wills put money into the infant Ford company, and was the first production manager. When, in 1919, Ford decided he wanted to exercise his whim of iron to the fullest, he bought out all his associates, and Wills became a multimillionaire then and there. He bought 4400 acres of Michigan land, built a plant and rolled the first automobile out of it in 1921.

This A-68 was first-cabin throughout, reflecting Wills's belief that a luxury automobile did not necessarily have to weigh three tons in order to be comfortable. He was a metallurgist, and liked molybdenum steel and aluminum as materials. The engine was reminiscent of the contemporary Hispano-Suiza, indeed, some thought derivative. The authorities Borgeson and Jaderquist think Wills's choice of a gray goose as a radiator emblem a shadow of the Hisso's flying stork, and Wills's method of acknowledging his indebtedness to Marc Birkigt. Derivative or not, the Wills Sainte Claire had much to recommend it, including a useful device even now available on very few cars: a cooling fan that cut out at speeds above 40 miles an hour, when a fan is unnecessary. The engine was a V-8. The 1921 depression probably prevented its making a place for itself, and Wills was out of business by the fall of 1922. He made a comeback the next year, but had to give up for good in 1927. An amusing touch on this roadster is a "courtesy light" on the left-hand side of the body, intended to give oncoming drivers a means of accurately gauging the width of the car.

MAXWELL

Year: *1923*
Model: *25*
Cylinders: *4*
Horsepower: *30*
Price: *$885*

Jonathan Dixon Maxwell set up the Maxwell-Briscoe Company in 1903. Maxwell was comparatively an old hand, having been in on the Haynes-Apperson car, and the Oldsmobile. Benjamin Briscoe was later to form the gigantic United States Motor Corporation, soaking up some 130 separate companies in the doing of it. Maxwell is credited with originating the thermo-syphon cooling system for automobiles, using the principle that heat rises to circulate water through an engine block without a mechanical pump. He made a twelve-cylinder flat-opposed engine in 1908.

Early Maxwells were standard for the time, in the two conventional body styles, roadster and touring car. They ran engines of 8 and 14 horsepower respectively. Maxwells covered a wide price range. A runabout could be had for $825, and the prestigious Model D limousine cost $3000. A Maxwell tied for first place in the 1905 Glidden Tour, and the make began to build up a considerable reputation in competition, even entering the Vanderbilt Cup races.

Briscoe left Maxwell in 1910 to fulfill his ambition to set up a company bigger than General Motors, but it failed within two years, and of all the entities involved, only Maxwell survived: the firm was reorganized as Maxwell-Briscoe in 1913 and went on making automobiles, and racing them when it could, twice at Indianapolis, for example, in 1914 and 1915, finishing ninth both times. Barney Oldfield drove a Maxwell at the Corona track in California in 1914, taking second place in a 300-mile race. In 1916 Maxwell leased part of the Chalmers plant in Detroit and the firm became Maxwell-Chalmers. In 1921 Walter Chrysler was brought in to reorganize the firm and shortly afterward he made it the hub of his own organization.

Because of the continuous references to the make on the Jack Benny radio show in the 1930's and 1940's, many more people living today have heard about Maxwell than have ever seen one. This particular Model B has a unique distinction. It was restored in 1962, and when Jack Benny appeared at Harrah's Club in Lake Tahoe, he drove the car, certainly the last, if not the only, Maxwell he ever did drive.

CHEVROLET

Year: *1923*
Model: *M*
Cylinders: *4*
Horsepower: *22*
Price: *$880*

The Chevrolet brothers, Louis-Joseph, Gaston and Arthur, were Swiss who grew up in France. They were racing drivers, mechanics, and Louis at least was an inventor: he had invented a wine-pump even before he came to the United States in 1900. The Chevrolets should have died millionaires, but then, so should David Dunbar Buick, of whom it was said that he made fifty fortunes—for other men—and so should William Crapo Durant, who organized General Motors, spent money as Kuwait sheiks are only said to do, and had assets of $250 when he went bankrupt in 1936.

Louis was the best driver of the Chevrolets and by 1905 he was in the big leagues. He beat the great Berner Eli Oldfield three times in 1905. He attracted W. C. Durant, a tiger who had been brought in to take over the Buick company and had shown how he operated by selling $500,000 worth of stock in one day. Durant hired Arthur Chevrolet as his chauffeur and Louis as a team driver for Buick. He did well. Two years later, Durant overextended General Motors by some $12,000,000 in the process of buying up other companies and was forced to resign. Louis Chevrolet went with him, and proposed that Durant set up to make a small car that he, Louis, would design. In November 1911, the Chevrolet Motor Company was formed, with Louis holding a major interest. The first product was a six-cylinder touring car at $2150. It was an immediate success and so was a cheaper model at $1475. One of the greatest business success stories in history had begun. Durant may have known it, but Louis Chevrolet did not. He had an argument with Durant (an easy thing to do) and Durant bought him out. Ironically, Louis went back to work for Chevrolet in 1934, twenty years later, and stayed with the firm until 1938, when ill health made him retire. He had a small pension. He died in 1941.

Chevrolet made an occasional oddball car down the years, and the copper-finned air-cooled model of 1923 was one of them. It was not esteemed, and nearly all the cars made were recalled. The Harrah specimen is one of only two known to be extant.

STUDEBAKER

Year: *1924*
Model: *EK Big 6*
Cylinders: *6*
Horsepower: *60/65*
Price: *$2685*

A seven-passenger sedan carrying every reasonable amenity: vanity case, smoking set, flower vase, jeweled 8-day clock and heater were all standard in this Studebaker, a mid-1920's product of a firm even then claiming to be the world's oldest manufacturer of highway vehicles. An indisputable claim, too, for while, say, Daimler-Benz had been making motorcars since the end of the nineteenth century, the Studebaker brothers began building wagons in 1852—and in South Bend, Indiana, still the home-place when passenger-car production was given up in 1964. The Studebakers had put wheels under people for more than a century.

There were five of them: Clem, Henry, Jacob, John Mohler and Peter. Clem and Henry started the business, basically a blacksmith shop, and made and sold three wagons in their first year. By 1856 they had a quietly good reputation for stout craftsmanship and drew a big plum: a U.S. Government contract for 100 wagons. By the time the Civil War came along the company was a major supplier. In 1874 somebody thought to time Studebaker's production: one carriage every seven minutes!

The Studebaker brothers were big, solid, bearded men, progressive in outlook but no wildcatters, and when they decided that the horse had probably had his day, and that they should begin to think about motors, they made it an electric, and kept right on producing horse-drawn carriages. In 1904, two years later, they added a gasoline-powered car, a two-cylin-

der tourer called the Studebaker-Garford (Garford chassis, Studebaker body) at $1250, but they kept on with the carriage business until they were perfectly sure the automobile was on a solid footing—in 1919. By that time, Studebaker was an industrial giant, with assets of many millions of dollars.

From the beginning to the end (the beautifully molded, dashing-looking, supercharged Avanti) Studebaker consistently kept an eye for what was new, stayed in front of the trends, and was never afraid of the big chance. Studebaker was the first to mass-produce an all-steel body, first to use a mechanical fuel pump, chrome-plating, free-wheeling, automatic spark control and a dozen other important processes or components. Studebaker executives authorized every kind of competition: Ab Jenkins ran a Commander Six sedan across the country in 77 hours, 40 minutes, in 1927 and Harry Hartz did 5000 miles in 4909 minutes at Culver City, California; in 1928 a President Eight did 30,000 miles in 26,329 minutes. A Studebaker was third at Indianapolis in 1932, and the firm ran *five* cars in 1933, a year in which it was officially broke, taking seventh, ninth, tenth, eleventh and twelfth places. Raymond Loewy's 1947 body design shook the industry to its shoes, and when in 1965 Brooks and William Stevens began to make the limited-production Excalibur SS, they used the Studebaker chassis. A splendid wagon, the Studebaker, from beginning to end.

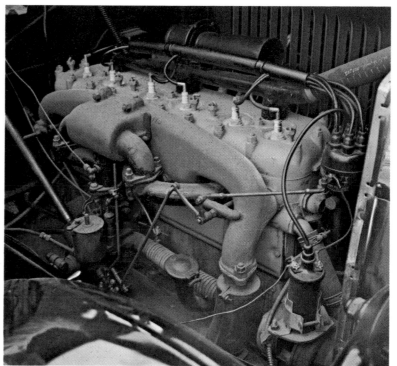

CHRYSLER

Year: *1924*
Model: *B*
Cylinders: *6*
Horsepower: *68*
Price: *$1395*

One of the best-looking of the Chrysler line, the Model B was a notable performer as well. The combination of a top speed of 70 miles an hour—fast for the 1920's—with four-wheel hydraulic brakes made the car a competent runner over winding roads in the hands of a good driver. For example, the racing driver Ralph de Palma took a Model B touring car up Mount Wilson in 25 minutes, 48 seconds, a run of 9½ miles through a rise of 4636 feet and 144 hard corners. The time was two minutes better than any stock car had previously done, and more than a minute better than the standing race-car record.

STAR

Year: *1925*
Model: *F*
Cylinders: *4*
Horsepower: *30*
Price: *$750*

There have been three Star automobiles, one British, two American, and this is the third in line, chronologically, the one made by Durant Motors, Incorporated. The Star was intended by Durant to be a competitor of the Ford and the Chevrolet—his own creation, of course, the Chevrolet, during his second tenure of the office of president of General Motors. He had lost control of the company in the crash of 1921, when GM stock dropped from $400 to $12 a share. He didn't miss a day of work, though, and by 1922 he had sold stock in Durant Motors to nearly 150,000 people and had more than $60,000,000 on the black side of the ledgers. Durant was one of the master salesmen and organizers of his or any other day. (One man, an admirer but no friend, said of him, "Billy could sell sifted sand to the Arabs. Hell, he could sell 'em *un*-sifted sand! And sieves the next day!") But he could not overcome the economic facts of life, which were that Ford and GM were too tough for a new product to buck in that day and age. By 1929 he was through.

This Star sedan, boxy and standard-looking, with its 50-MPH top speed, is thus another in the list of milestone cars, remarkable not so much for themselves as for their places in history.

BENTLEY

Year: *1925*
Model: *3–Litre*
Cylinders: *4*
Horsepower: *70*
Price: *$6500*

Bentley motorcars were turned out with radiator badges in red, black, blue or green enamel, and these designations sometimes, but not always today, identify the car by model. They are invariably called "labels" by Bentley enthusiasts—thus, "He has a Red-label tourer"—although the factory term was "badge." In any case, this is a green-badge Bentley, and genuine, thus identified as one of the fifteen 3-Litre short-chassis models made particularly for racing.

The 24-Hour Race at Le Mans was won five times by Bentley cars, a record until Jaguar and Ferrari came along after World War II. One of these victories, in 1927, resulted in an automobile being guest of honor at a dinner at the historic Savoy Hotel in London. The car was the 3-Litre Bentley called by the team "Old No. 7" and it had won the 1927 Le Mans race after the accident that has probably been more talked over and written about than any other automobile accident in history: the Crash at White House Corner. It happened during the night. There were three Bentleys entered that year, and at 9:30 one of them was running a little way ahead of the other two. This car came around White House Corner around 90 MPH to find a French car that had spun and stalled halfway across the road. The Bentley missed it, hit the ditch, rolled, and ended half-across the road in its turn. The second Bentley crashed into it. The third, Old No. 7, was in the hands of the great driver-journalist S. C. H. Davis, and something, a flash of headlight as a car rolled, or gravel on the road, warned him enough for him to reduce his speed by 20 miles an hour. He hit the first Bentley, broke a wheel, bent the front axle, put the steering out of line, knocked out a headlight, bent the frame, and lost a good deal of braking capability. But he stuck things together as best he could (the rules of the time required drivers to do their own repairs), the car ran until three o'clock the next afternoon, and won the race.

JORDAN

Year: *1926*
Model: *J*
Cylinders: *8*
Horsepower: *64*
Price: *$1695*

Edward S. Jordan, known to the trade as Ned, made automobiles in Cleveland, Ohio, from 1918 to 1930. His early models were sound if unspectacular, some of them flamboyantly named, like the Great Jordan Line Eight, but it was this car, the Playboy model, that assured him a permanent place in any listing of the titans of the industry. The Playboy was worth all of the $1695 it cost. Useful thought had gone into it: the upholstery was removable for cleaning—and to allow a body-shop to push out dents—such conveniences as automatic windshield wipers and a transmission lock were standard, and the car was fast for its time. But it was not the car that made Jordan's name, it was the advertisement with which he announced it, the famous "Somewhere West of Laramie" copy which is still cited as the most influential motorcar advertisement of all time:

> Somewhere west of Laramie there's a broncho-busting, steer-roping girl who knows what I'm talking about. She can tell what a sassy pony, that's a cross between greased lightning and the place where it hits, can do with eleven hundred pounds of steel and action when he's going high, wide and handsome.
>
> The truth is—the Playboy was built for her.
>
> Built for the lass whose face is brown with the sun when the day is done of revel and romp and race.
>
> She loves the cross of the wild and the tame.
>
> There's a savor of links about that car—of laughter and lilt and light—a hint of old loves—and saddle and quirt. It's a brawny thing—yet a graceful thing for the sweep o' the Avenue.
>
> Step into the Playboy when the hour grows dull with things gone dead and stale.
>
> Then start for the land of real living with the spirit of the lass who rides, lean and rangy, into the red horizon of a Wyoming twilight.

The root idea behind this advertisement was fundamental to the concept of forced obsolescence that has made the United States economy the richest in the world. It recognized that sales appeals based on horsepower, gear ratios, top speeds and the like reached only a small group of knowledgeable people, either already converted or inclined to be disputatious. Far better to suggest that possession of the product would somehow magically transform the buyer, surround him with an aura of romance, make him happier in every way. Jordan's idea has sold everything from shredded coconut to cigarettes, and, of course, automobiles. Buick's early 1965 campaign for the Riviera was a direct lineal descendant of Jordan's Playboy ad: "Drive a Riviera home tonight. Who cares if people think you're younger, richer and more romantic than you really are?"

RICKENBACKER

Year: *1926*
Model: *Series E Famous 6*
Cylinders: *6*
Horsepower: *68*
Price *$1795*

Edward V. Rickenbacker has lived a full life, race-driver, World War I flying ace, race-track promoter on the grand scale (Indianapolis), central figure in one of the legendary survival stories of World War II, airline president, and automobile manufacturer. He was a success at everything he undertook except the last-named endeavor, a cruelly short-lived one.

Rickenbacker did not design the car that bore his name; his role was that of prestige-bearer and promoter. The car was, if not extraordinarily distinguished, still as good as most of its contemporaries, and notable as one of the early users of four-wheel brakes. In the beginning days of the motorcar, it seemed logical to brake the rear wheels only, as the wagon-makers did, even if they used only the "sprag," the scoop-like device that, dropped under the wheel, caused it to drag. Later, when speeds outran braking power, the driveshaft was attacked with a view to reducing speed independently of the wheels. This was never really effective. In 1909, a Dutch car, the Spyker, appeared with brakes on all four wheels. British designers were quick to pick it up, and in 1911 the Isotta-Fraschini of Italy had them. Still, although the system was not generally accepted until the middle 1920's, Rickenbacker's use of it was no radical notion. But it was new enough on the American market to allow the competition to get in some effective counter-propaganda, the shrewdest stroke being the argument that it was absolute madness to apply braking power to the same wheels that steered the car: loss of control was almost certain to result, the story ran. The fact of the matter is, of course, that braking force applied to the front wheels, so long as it is applied evenly, has no effect on control, and because the effect of braking is to transfer weight to the front of the automobile, front-wheel brakes are more effective than rear-wheel. But too many people chose to believe what they heard, and did not wish to be confused by truth. Other factors obtained in the case of the Rickenbacker, of course, but certainly its "radical" braking system did it no good, and the make lived only six years, from 1922 to 1927.

AMILCAR

Year: *1926*
Model: *Series CGSs*
Cylinders: *4*
Horsepower: *35*
Price: *$1400*

Frenchmen and Englishmen who liked to race in the 1920's and 1930's were devoted to the Amilcar, and for good reason: it was one of the best cheap race cars we have had. Shown here is a classic of the line, the CGSs, in which bit of nomenclature the "C" meant it was a Type C, the "GS" stood for Grand Sport and the "s" for Surbaisse, the name by which this model was usually known. It cost $1400, weighed fewer pounds than that, and would do 75 miles an hour, which, while no blistering speed even in 1926, was, with good handling, quite enough to win races in the Amilcar's competition class. The "Surbaisse" had excellent brakes for its day and an endearing gasoline consumption: better than 40 miles to the gallon.

The word "Amilcar" was coined, being a loose anagram of the name of one of its originators, M. Lamy, plus "car," and it was first heard in 1921. The car won first time out, at the Bol d'Or, like Le Mans a 24-hour race, run over a shorter (three-mile) circuit. The Amilcar engine was designed for the 1100-cubic centimeter class, and the first one was 200 cc's under that figure. Later models came up to 1094 cc, beginning with the six-cylinder of 1926, a miniature grand prix machine that could put out 80 horsepower and 100 miles an hour. Indeed one of them once did 115.54 MPH for an hour, marking a new world record, and in 1926 an Amilcar Six was second overall—to a 1500-cc. Bugatti—in the British Junior Car Club's 200-Mile race.

Few companies have been able to make the production of sports and competition cars richly rewarding, and Amilcar, around 1930, elected to try to make more money with big passenger cars, using straight-eight engines. But people who remembered the old racing Amilcars were not amused, and too few newcomers came along.

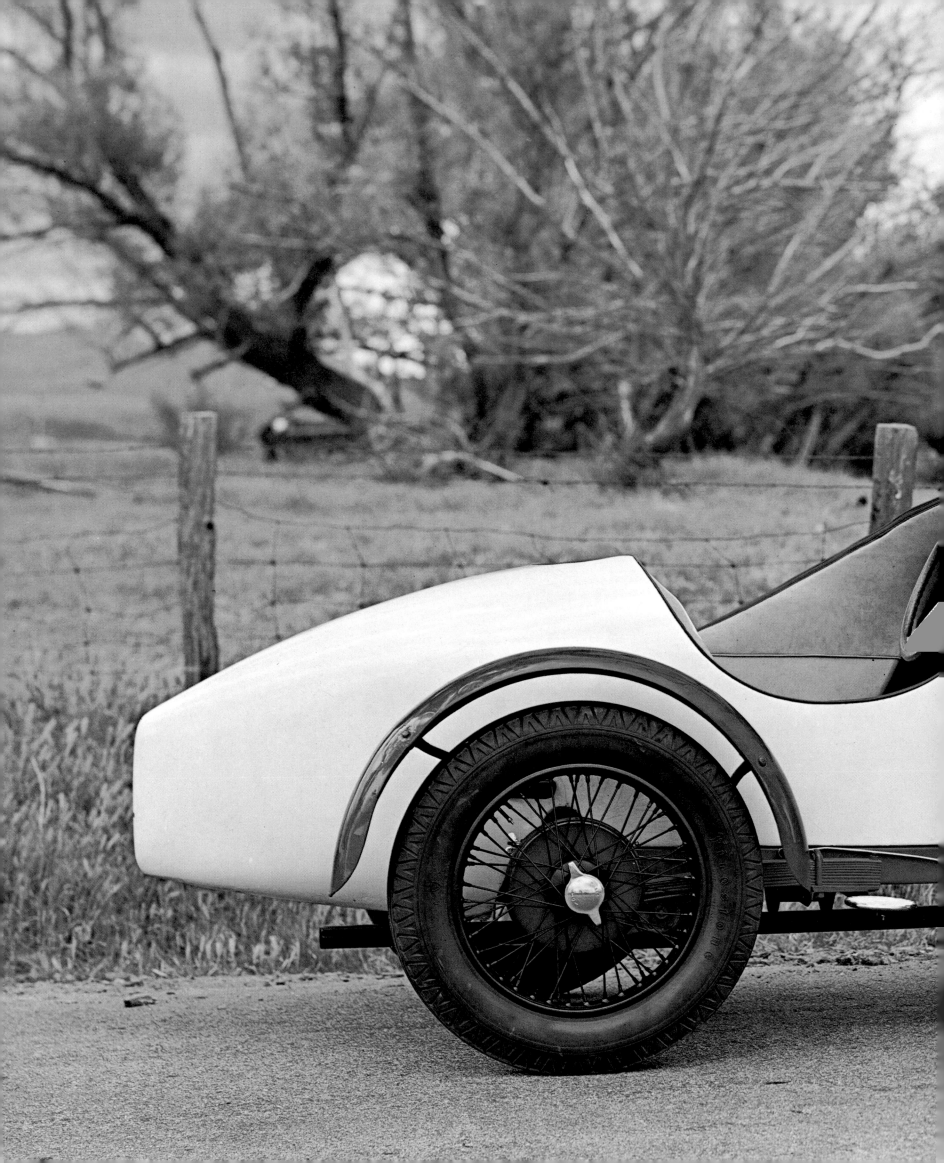

BUGATTI

Year: *1926*
Model: *Type 23*
Cylinders: *4*
Horsepower: *40*
Price: *$3000*

Ettore Bugatti was an Italian who lived nearly all his life in France among Frenchmen, and he was, as we say, a character, an exotic, one of a kind, greatly gifted, proud, unswervingly independent, indifferent to any opinion but his own, amused, aristocratic, impractical, profligate, a connoisseur, a gourmet, a bon vivant. He died in 1947 after sixty-six years of life full of frenzy and creation. He made automobiles from 1910 to 1939. He made comparatively few: only about 7500 units, in approximately forty-five basic models. The location, ownership and condition of more than 1100 of them are known today, and there are probably another 100 still undiscovered—an extraordinarily high proportion of survival when it is considered that France went through two major wars in the factory's lifetime.

Bugatti used varying terminology for his cars, and numbered them by type, the whole roster running from Type 13 to Type 102, but not consecutively. This one is a Type 23, otherwise called a Brescia, properly a Brescia Modifié, after a racing model that made a re-

markable success in the 1921 Italian Grand Prix, run that year in Brescia. The body is called an Opera Coupé, seats three people, and was built by the coachbuilder Gastom Grummer on the Weymann principle: a wooden frame carefully insulated from the chassis and covered with leather. Weymann bodies were somewhat vulnerable, but they were nearly squeak-proof. The windshield was split horizontally and the top half could be opened. This was a device useful in heavy fog, in the days before interior heating and effective wipers were commonplace.

The Bugatti was an expensive motorcar, and attracted custom coachwork, so that, the racing cars aside, there is no such thing as a "standard" Bugatti body. However, excepting the cars built before 1913, all Bugatti radiator shells are uniformly shaped, variations on a form which has been likened variously to that of an arch, a pear, a horseshoe. Whatever it looks like, it is unique among the thousands of radiator designs that have been made, and consistently beautiful.

MERCEDES

Year: *1927*
Model: *K*
Cylinders: *6*
Horsepower: *100/140*
Price: *$10,500*

Gottlieb Daimler ran a four-wheeled gasoline-pro-pelled vehicle on public roads in 1887; Karl Benz had driven his in the autumn of 1885, and their joint claim to the invention of the automobile, to the extent that any single individual can be said to have invented it, is very strong, although they never met. The name of the Daimler product was changed to Mercedes in 1900 as a result of a financial interest taken in the firm by a wealthy Austrian, Emile Jellinek, Austro-Hungarian consul at Nice. Jellinek was given the Daimler con-cession for all of France, and stipulated that since a German name would be no help in sales—people still remembered the war of 1870—the car should be called Mercedes, after one of his daughters. This first Mer-cedes has been cited the first really modern motorcar: it had a honeycomb radiator in front, a gate gearshift, an accurate throttle control, at the time an absolute innovation, and it was remarkably quiet. In 1926 the two firms were merged to become Daimler-Benz Ak-tiengesellschaft, and the cars were called Mercedes-Benz. The company can now claim to be the oldest manufactory of motorcars in the world, and certainly one of the most successful.

The Model K touring car was designed by Fer-dinand Porsche, and is notable primarily as the root ancestor of the models immediately following it, the S, SS, SSK and SSKL cars which set up an almost unparalleled series of triumphs in sports-car racing all over the world during the late 1920's and early 1930's. It was, taken by itself, no success. Advertised to do 100 miles an hour, it would usually not quite reach 90, its handling qualities at high speed were frightening, and vintage car authorities, in discussing its brakes, usually fall back on terms such as "unmentionable" or "ter-rifying." It was supercharged in Mercedes-Benz's unique system: a Roots-type blower, normally idle, was cut in by a clutch on full depression of the accelerator, and blew air *through* the carburetor, setting up a satisfy-ing siren-like scream, and, somewhat theoretically, increasing the horsepower from 100 to 140.

132

STUTZ

Year: *1927*
Model: *Series AA Blackhawk*
Cylinders: *8*
Horsepower: *95*
Price: *$4895*

In 1926, the Stutz company radically altered its purpose, which had been the production of fast and fairly hairy motorcars, and began to emphasize instead the more elegant qualities. The new Stutzes were quiet by prevailing standards, the bodies fitted out with best leather and solid black walnut. The engine used an overhead camshaft, and the brakes were hydraulic. They sounded chancy—the hydraulic pressure expanded little rubber bags which moved the brake shoes—but they worked well if they were carefully maintained. This was a heavy car, at 4340 pounds, and a costly one.

NASH

Year: *1927*
Model: *236*
Cylinders: *6*
Horsepower: *52*
Price: *$1225*

Charles W. Nash was a pleasant person, a gentleman, a man of taste, and so obviously all these things that they plainly stand out in photographs made of him in his middle years and later. He was the kind of man who was happy to be able to say that in a long marriage he and his wife had been apart for ten days on only two occasions. He had been a hard worker all his life, bound-boy to a farmer when he was six years old. He was a major figure in Detroit affairs long before the Kaiser War: president of Buick, Oakland, Olds. In 1912 he was president of General Motors. He resigned in 1916, following the inevitable donnybrook with Billy Durant—although he told the veteran Detroit reporter David Wilkie that he was ashamed to mention the amount of the salary Durant offered him to stay on: "No man is worth that much." But Nash had always wanted to make his own car, and so he left.

The company he took over was the Jeffery Company of Kenosha, Wisconsin, producers of buggy-autos, and then the Rambler, beginning in 1909. There were two bright little spots in the company's history: the Jeffery had persuaded the *Saturday Evening Post* to run the first American advertisement showing a woman openly smoking a cigarette—it was a Chesterfield—and the Rambler had in 1909 startled the nation with the offer of a fifth, or "spare" wheel, as an optional extra at from $75 to $85.

The Nash company was thoroughly progressive. It was one of the first to offer unitized body construction, had rubber-mounted engines in 1922 (cf. Plymouth). A merger with Kelvinator came in 1936, bringing in George Mason, and the new company absorbed Hudson in 1954 as American Motors. Nash was quick to recognize the Italian dominance of body-styling after World War II and for some time maintained a contract with Pinin Farina. There was perhaps never a really bad Nash; some were better than others. The company was famous in the trade as exceptionally well-run. Even in the ultra-depression year of 1931, Nash, next to General Motors, had the best financial position, and the highest profit, in the industry.

FALCON-KNIGHT

Year: *1928*
Model: *12*
Cylinders: *6*
Horsepower: *45*
Price: *$1250*

The Falcon-Knight was not long with us and it left no permanent mark on the industry except as one of the motorcars to use the Knight sleeve-valve engine. This was an alternative to the standard poppet-valve arrangement. It limited engine speed, used a great deal of oil, and made an overhaul very complicated, but it was silent in the extreme, and thus attractive to makers of luxury cars like Minerva and Daimler.

This Falcon-Knight special de luxe roadster was remarkable in that rumble-seat riders did not have to get wet as a matter of course: the auxiliary top was standard equipment. It was probably the only genuine consideration shown for rumble-seat riders until the postwar British Triumph drophead coupé came along. On that car, part of the rumble-seat lid lifted and turned itself into a windshield.

DIANA

Year: *1928*
Model: *880*
Cylinders: *8*
Horsepower: *72*
Price: *$1795*

A transitory make of the middle 1920's (1925–1928), the Diana was made by the Moon company of St. Louis and is thus related distantly to the Ruxton, the Gardner and the Kissel, as well as to the Moon. The Diana used the Continental Series 127 engine, which would move it (at a hair under 3000 pounds) to 71 miles an hour. The Diana had the advanced Ross steering gear, on the strength of which it was billed as the easiest-steering car in America, and the Lanchester damper, a British patent, to smooth out the engine. It was one of the earliest users of Lockheed hydraulic brakes, and the Moon people argued that its acceleration was notable: 5 to 25 MPH in 6.5 seconds. Today, the car is remembered not for any of its mechanical features but for the fully sculptured figure of Diana, complete with bow, arrows and dog, which formed the radiator ornament.

BUGATTI

Year: *1928*
Model: *Type 37A*
Cylinders: *4*
Horsepower: *90*
Price: *$3525*

Like Ferdinand Porsche and Enzo Ferrari, Ettore Bugatti ran the whole range of automobile design: he made passenger, sports, and racing cars. His race cars were spectacularly successful; they were the world's standard, and their record stood untouched for years, indeed until quite recent times, when Ferrari eclipsed it. A measure of Bugatti preeminence: in the years 1926 and 1927, a total of 1049 victories! Typically, he made what is still thought to be the most beautiful race car of all time, the Type 35, and he made one that has an equally valid claim to being the ugliest, the almost unspeakably grotesque 2-liter grand prix car of 1923.

This one, the Type 37A, is a variation on the Type 35 theme. It has four cylinders (except for one 16-cylinder, Bugatti engines were all fours or eights) and a small supercharger. Its top speed was generally held to be around 110 miles an hour, but carefully prepared models could be made to go faster, and a record of 122 MPH was made at the Brooklands track in England before World War II.

Bugatti race cars showed notable peculiarities of design. Like so many great innovators, Bugatti was radical in some ways, reactionary in others. When he came upon a good thing, he was loath to leave it. He liked a spring design called reversed one-quarter elliptic, and every race car he built carried it. He made a startlingly good wheel for his cars, of aluminum alloy with the brake drum cast integrally, so that when a car, halfway through a race, came into the pits for new tires, it got new brakes as well, but almost to the end of his productive life he refused to specify hydraulic brakes, using the out-of-date cable system. He would not use superchargers until necessity forced him, holding that while they were mechanically efficient, they were morally wrong, because by *forcing* air into the cylinders, instead of allowing them to aspirate it normally, a supercharger illegally increased engine capacity!

Bugatti began life as an artist, and his cars showed it clearly. (He used to say that he would not employ even a draftsman who could not draw in perspective, in the round.) The components of his cars, things like gearshift and brake levers, were always aesthetically pleasing, and his steering wheels remain to this day the most beautiful ever drawn. A Bugatti engine looks like no other in the world: everything possible inside, not outside, a straight-sided, straight-topped structure, and the metal itself usually "flaked," or lightly chased, square centimeter by centimeter, by hand. The instrument panels of his racing cars were engine-turned, like the inside of a cigarette case. Even the vises in his factory were enameled and polished.

CUNNINGHAM

Year: *1928*
Model: *V7*
Cylinders: *8*
Horsepower: *106*
Price: *$8000*

James Cunningham, a sturdy Scots-Irishman, came to the United States in 1833 and settled in Rochester, New York. He found work with the coachbuilding firm of Hanford & Whitbeck, and in 1838 formed a partnership with two other employees and bought the company, which concentrated on cutters and buggies. In 1842 Cunningham bought out his partners, and by the 1890's the firm was making four-fifths of all the carriages sold west of the Mississippi River. Cunningham coaches were of the first grade. In 1908 the firm began to make motorcars on a custom basis, while continuing to make fine horse-drawn carriages as well. The Cunningham was one of the best cars money could buy—and it took money: prices began at $6500. There were no stock bodies catalogued: the client could have what he liked, and what he could pay for.

This was a car for the discriminating, big, solid, running a huge V–8 engine (471 cubic inches) with rear main bearings almost four inches long. Production was limited, at a rate of perhaps fifty cars a year, an estimated five hundred total from 1924 until the company stopped production around 1930. (In 1936, they made a small town car on the Ford V–8 chassis. A Ford sedan at the time cost $655, but with a Cunningham coupé-de-ville body it was billed at $2600!) The company is still under Cunningham control in the fourth generation, making various industrial products. One of the few other Rochester-built Cunninghams is in the collection of Briggs Cunningham, who built a very fast sports-racing car (no relation) in the 1950's which for a time dominated U.S. racing and was twice third in the Le Mans 24-Hour Race.

ESSEX

Year: *1929*
Model: *Super Six*
Cylinders: *6*
Horsepower: *55*
Price: *$945*

The Essex was not a distinguished automobile, stylistically or mechanically, but it did achieve at least one gold star in the roll of history: the 1926 Essex Coach at $765 offered such remarkable value—it was really the first closed car sold at a price competitive with the open cars of the time—that it brought the great Henry Ford to think long and hard about a replacement for his Model T.

Essex was a Hudson product, made by a company named after its financier, Joseph L. Hudson, wealthy through a Detroit department store, although the moving spirit in the organization was Roy Chapin. Chapin's place in the spaghetti-like genealogy chart of American automobilism begins when he was an assistant of sorts to R. E. Olds. The Hudson "20" was the first car of the name, and by 1916, the firm had a legitimate position as an innovator in high-speed engine design, the "Super Six" of that year being a big winner in stock-car races.

I am inclined to believe, although I cannot prove the contention, that the only car that has ever been represented on a coin, a sedan shown on the silver *yuan* of Kweichow Province, 1931, is an Essex. The Kweichow *yuan* used to be available at any rare coin shop for a couple of dollars; having given a number of them away as presents years ago, I am reluctant to learn what they have come to be worth since 1945.

Essex disappeared as a separate entity of Hudson in 1931, and the parent company was absorbed in American Motors in 1954. Hudson went out in a burst of glory, though, practically unbeatable on the stock-car circuits. This "Speedabout" body, by Biddle & Smart, is not typical of the square, boxlike sedans that made the Essex name.

CHRYSLER

Year: *1929*
Model: *Imperial 80*
Cylinders: *6*
Horsepower: *100*
Price: *$2995*

The Chrysler Building in New York, an architectural landmark for all time, stands to the memory of a man whose first concern with machinery was as an engine-wiper on a railroad, Walter P. Chrysler. He went into the industry with Buick in 1911, was one of the key executives brought into the fledgling General Motors by the sharp-eyed William Durant, and stayed until 1920, at a fantastic salary, until the inevitable quarrel with the hair-triggered Durant. He was engaged— "hired" seems hardly the word, considering that he was paid $1,000,000 a year for the task—to pull Willys-Overland out of trouble. It took him two years and he moved to Maxwell-Chalmers, bought the firm and dropped Chalmers.

The Chrysler Corporation began business in 1924, a good year, and sold $50,000,000 worth of automobiles in the first twelve months of its existence, a record then and now. The first Chrysler had six cylinders, a 70-horsepower high-compression engine and four-wheel hydraulic brakes. Chrysler products have always been marked by sound engineering and production practice, and to demonstrate this, two of them were run in the 1928 24-Hour Race at Le Mans, widely held by experts, then as now, to be a contest in which only European-built machinery had a chance of success. They finished third and fourth, astonishing placement, and in the same year another Chrysler took second at Spa in Belgium.

Elegant coachwork was erected on Chrysler chassis by Dietrich, Le Baron and Locke. This convertible coupé was one of three body styles done by Locke for the factory. It lacked few refinements. For example, in most rumble-seat models of the day, the postillion riders had to mount over the side of the car. The Chrysler by Locke, like the Rolls-Royce, had a door to make the enterprise less like climbing into the back window of a house after one has lost the key. Glass was the new shatterproof type. Upholstery was to the client's taste. In 1928 the De Soto line was added, and the Plymouth, memorable for its successful adaptation of the rubber engine-mounting system pioneered in Europe. It was something remarkable, to see the little Plymouth engine twisting like a live thing as power went on and off.

KISSEL

Year: *1929*
Model: *White Eagle 126*
Cylinders: *8*
Horsepower: *126*
Price: *$3275*

Detroit may be the automobile capital of the world, but there are people in Wisconsin who'll argue that it was only by accident that the mantle didn't fall on Milwaukee. Indeed, there was a time when Wisconsin seemed well in the lead. Eighty-odd makes of cars and trucks were produced in the state; of the automobiles, only Nash survives. Wisconsin claims the first road race in the world, in 1878, when, in competition for $10,000 put up by the state legislature, two steam wagons ran from Green Bay to Madison, the winner allegedly doing the distance at the blistering rate of 6 miles an hour. The Carhart steamer is dated at 1872, and the Schloemer gasoline car at 1889.

Nash aside, the best-remembered Wisconsin-made motorcar is the Kissel, which began life as the Kisselkar around 1906. The Kissel company was always a small family enterprise, probably never had more than a thousand workers on the payroll. Unlike many such operations, Kissel made its own engines, but produced few innovations. One of them was useful, and created a stir at the time: the removable hardtop body, which Kissel first offered in 1915, and later patented, although the basic principle had been used long before. The idea was a sound one, and is still used in some sports cars today: you hooked a block-and-tackle to the hardtop, loosened a few fastenings, and hauled the thing up to the garage roof, to stay there until cold weather returned. A cloth top replaced it. Another novelty was an extra seat which pulled out from the body above the running board on each side. These seats were for brave people and perhaps accounted for the vaudeville joke: "How can you tell a happy motorist?" "That's easy — by the bugs in his teeth!"

The White Eagle model shown here and the sporty-looking Gold Bug were the best-known Kissels. The company abandoned its six-cylinder engines in 1925 in favor of straight-eights, but couldn't weather the Depression, and gave up in 1931.

150

ROOSEVELT

Year: *1929*
Model: *S*
Cylinders: *8*
Horsepower: *70*
Price: *$995*

A stout-hearted attempt by the Marmon company to break into the low-price market was the Roosevelt, urged on a not conspicuously eager public as the first straight-eight automobile to be sold under $1000. It was named after President Theodore Roosevelt, who had died in 1919, and carried an excellent likeness of him, in profile, on its radiator badge. (Some historians believe that Roosevelt was the first President to ride in a motorcar in public, in 1907, in Lansing, Michigan, R. E. Olds at the wheel.) The car was, if publicity could be believed, as audacious and as dashing as Teddy himself had been, rushing up San Juan Hill the hard way, but it did not, somehow, succeed in making that impression generally.

GRAHAM-PAIGE

Year: *1929*
Model: *837*
Cylinders: *8*
Horsepower: *123*
Price: *$2195*

This was a *de luxe* item in the Graham-Paige line; six wire wheels were standard equipment and the gearbox was four-speed, with a high-ratio rear axle. The body is by Le Baron. The Graham-Paige company succeeded Paige-Detroit, and dropped the "Paige" the year this car was built. Graham introduced skirted fenders to the American market in 1932. The make had a British cousin, the Lammas-Graham, a super-charged sports car, and a Lammas-Graham won the last race held at the famous Brooklands circuit, in August 1939. The make finally disappeared into the Kaiser-Frazer combination.

LA SALLE

Year: *1929*
Model: *328*
Cylinders: *8*
Horsepower: *86*
Price: *$2395*

The roots of General Motors's absolute preeminence as an industrial success are many, and among them is the shrewdness with which the components of the various makes under the company's big roof are stirred up to create new models and even new entities. The La Salle, a good if undistinguished motorcar, is remarkable only for its short life—1927 to 1940—and the fact that there really never was a La Salle. The first one was impossible to tell from a Cadillac unless one looked into the engine, which was smaller by a bit, or got close enough to see the nameplate. The bodies, by Fisher or Fleetwood, were identical. In 1934 the modified Cadillac engine was dropped and a stock Oldsmobile eight-cylinder put in, to the accompaniment of a rousing cut in price to put the car into the same price bracket as the small Packard. In 1937, a slightly smaller-than-standard Cadillac Series 60 V–8 went back into the La Salle, and it was still running this engine when production was discontinued early in the war years. General Motors had created three cars simply by reaching into the parts-bins. The La Salles were splendid value for money, good-looking, fast and comfortable. They looked and felt big. The name was that of the redoubtable French explorer, René Robert La Salle, who claimed the whole Mississippi Valley for France and was killed by his own men on an expedition in 1687. His contemporary, Antoine de la Mothe Cadillac, was the founder of Detroit.

154

AUBURN

Year: *1929*
Model: *8-90S*
Cylinders: *8*
Horsepower: *100*
Price: *$1495*

We think of the Auburns as cars of the 1930's, but the firm was in existence in 1900. It produced nothing of significance until it became part of E. L. Cord's four-cornered empire: Auburn, Cord, Duesenberg, Lycoming, in 1924. There can have been few motorcars in history as good as the Auburn, and as good-looking, that sold for so little money. Unlike so many cars much esteemed in their own time, Auburns are esthetically quite acceptable today, most of them, splendidly balanced arrangements of mass and line, and by modern standards they are capable of adequate parkway performance, too.

The "new" Auburn line began in 1925, the year of the first Lycoming-engined car. Five years later, the price was $400 less and the horsepower 83 per cent higher. One more year, and Auburn was in striking distance of the top ten sales position: in 1931 the firm was thirteenth overall, ahead of such formidable runners as De Soto, Hudson and Packard. The Model 8-88 Auburn set thirty-four unlimited stock-car speed records at distances from 5 to 15,000 miles. Most Auburns would approach 100 miles an hour, and in 1932 a V–12 Speedster did 100.77 for a mile, 92.16 for 100 miles, and 88.95 for 500.

The boat-tailed Auburn roadsters were svelte, chic-looking two-seaters, much admired by the bloods of the day, particularly those on the supercharged 8 and the V–12 chassis. I remember seeing the late Sam Collier, who, with his brother Miles, Cameron Argetsinger, Jr., and Alec Ulmann revived American road racing after World War II, running majestically into a little Massachusetts town in a boat-tail, towing a race car, altogether a splendid *equipe*. It may have been the introduction of the V–12 that killed off the Auburn, ironically. Some authorities believe it was priced too low at well under $2000: people in the market for V–12 automobiles suspected that a really good one couldn't cost so little.

DUESENBERG

Year: *1929*
Model: *J*
Cylinders: *8*
Horsepower: *265*
Price: *$14,000*

The dual-cowl phaeton body was a rarity even in the golden age of coachbuilding because it could properly be placed on a long chassis only; it was profligate in its use of space. One saw dual-cowls only on the likes of Cadillac, Packard, Lincoln and Duesenberg chassis, and of all of them the Duesenberg was most esteemed. This one is by Murphy of Pasadena. It was a whimsy of some owners to specify extra instruments in these carriages, so that the folk in the rear seat, cut off from a view of the pilot's panel, could tell when the car was coming up to its maximum of 115 miles an hour or so. One of the niceties of standard Duesenberg instrumentation was a set of four red and green lights which told the driver when the automatic chassis-lubrication system was operating, when to change the oil—every 750 miles—and when to add water to the battery.

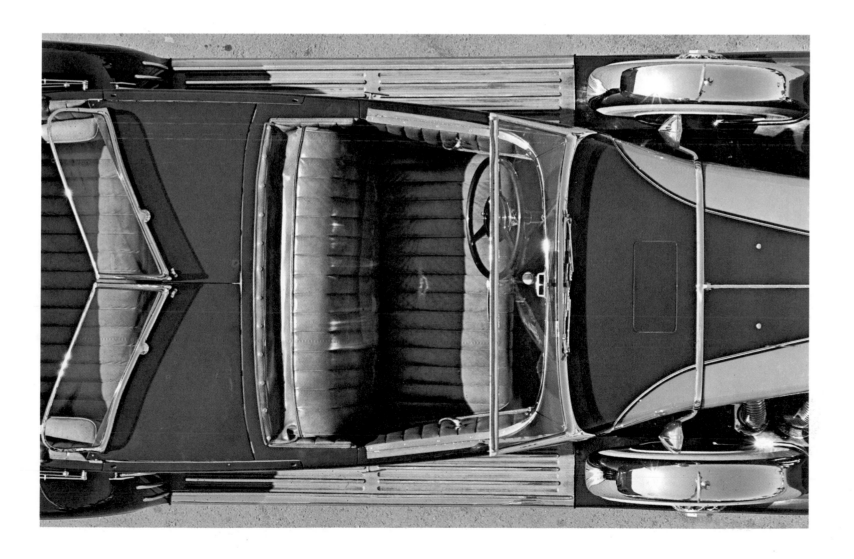

DU PONT

Year: *1930*
Model: *G*
Cylinders: *8*
Horsepower: *130*
Price: *$5750*

The Du Pont family—it seems a thin word to describe empire-builders—have been unused to failures, but the automobile bearing the name was only, if that, a *succès d'éstime*. This example of the make, however, catalogued as a "Royal Town Car," was certainly first-cabin in every particular, and had the benefit of a restoration, by Jack Nethercutt of Los Angeles, that brought it to mint condition before it came into the hands of Harrah's people.

The Du Pont company began to make automobiles around 1921, and in 1929 it did a rather audacious thing: it sent a car to Le Mans. Motoring writers of the time described the body as beautiful, but cited the car overall as too heavy for its power, and unproven under sustained high-speed conditions. It went out with gearbox failure before it had done two hundred miles. That was a Bentley year—first, second, third, fourth places—but a Stutz and two Chryslers were next in line. Du Pont ran a car at Indianapolis in 1930, but it was hopelessly slow and would, on form, have finished dead last had it not crashed on the twenty-second lap.

This coupé de ville is one of only 125 Du Ponts made in 1930. The body, by Merrimac, is in the classic mold. Admirable, in my view, is the privacy it affords. A limousine of similar excellence today is sheeted with plate glass on all sides, as if to put the occupants on exhibition. Often, in the evening traffic of any of the great cities of the West, one sees a chauffeur-driven Cadillac, Rolls-Royce, Rover, Citroën, Mercedes-Benz, its single tycoon-type passenger reading, always reading, while people on crosswalks very nearly look over his shoulder. (In England, in a Rover or a Van den Plas Princess, he will be reading under the light of a flexible-neck hooded lamp sold as an accessory, practical and quite elegant.) This wanton exposure seems to me ridiculous if not vulgar. A town car should have one window in each door, in the rear a glass oval six inches long—and that's all.

DUESENBERG

Year: *1930*
Model: *J*
Cylinders: *8*
Horsepower: *265*
Price: *$13,500*

The only American automobile ever to win a European grand prix race was a Duesenberg, the Grand Prix of France, in 1921, driven by Jimmy Murphy. The Duesenberg may have been the finest automobile made in this country, and although the last one was sold in 1937, the mark left on American consciousness by the Duesenberg was so deep and lasting that in 1965 a company was formed to make a new Duesenberg, like the old one a great luxury motorcar, if not, like the old one, a great racing car. Fritz Duesenberg, son of August Duesenberg and nephew of Fred, is chairman of the board.

The Duesenberg brothers, German-born, came to America in the 1880's. Fred became a race driver, designed a car—it was called the Mason—in 1904, and in 1913 he and August formed the Duesenberg Motor Company to make race cars. They entered two in the 1914 Indianapolis 500, finishing tenth and fourteenth, with Eddie Rickenbacker in the first car. By 1920 their cars were fast enough to take the world's land speed record at 156 miles an hour. They began to make pas-

senger cars, showing the Model A first in November 1920. The Duesenberg "A" was the first U.S. passenger car to have four-wheel hydraulic brakes (they really *were* hydraulic; the operating fluid was water). It was the first to use molybdenum steel in the chassis, the first to use ground instead of cast transmission gears—the list is a long one.

In 1929 the Duesenberg Model J appeared, offering an engine with the then astounding horsepower of 265. It was expensive, $8500 for the bare chassis, and worth it. On this chassis all the great coachbuilders erected lavish and beautiful bodies: Murphy, Rollston, Le Baron, Hibbard & Darrin, Bohman & Schwartz. Here we have a club sedan by Murphy, who did some 125 bodies for the factory. The Duesenberg was *the* status symbol of the day, and its advertising was possibly the most restrained in the industry's history. Typical: a drawing of a patrician-looking gentleman at the wheel of a racing yacht, or sitting in his library listening to a pipe-organ of cathedral size, with the single line: "He drives a Duesenberg."

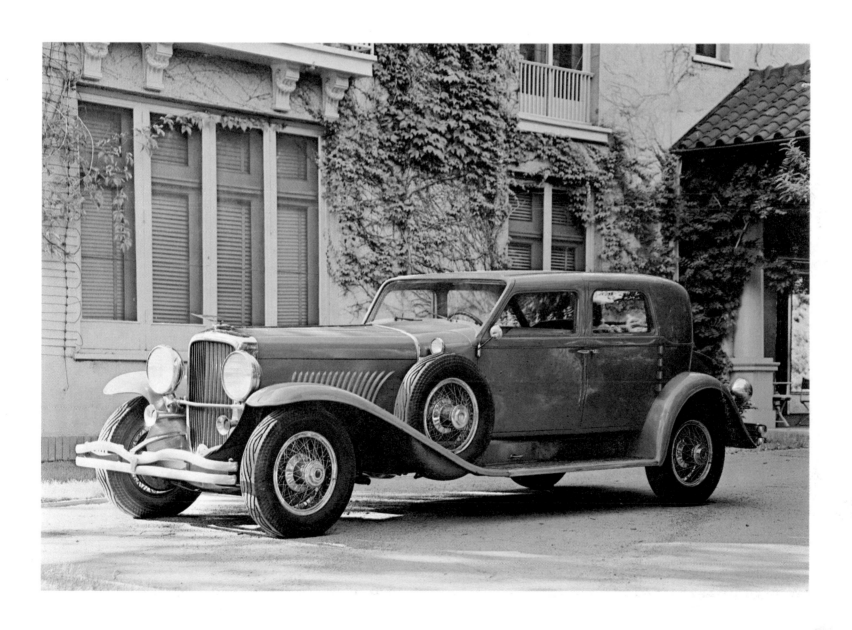

PACKARD

Year: *1930*
Model: *734*
Cylinders: *8*
Horsepower: *145*
Price: *$5200*

This Speedster Runabout is a favorite of the many Packards in the Harrah Collection, one of approximately 125 of these boat-tail roadsters produced. About sixteen of them are known to exist today. Customers had a full choice of color scheme in the Speedster Runabouts, and this one was done in what the factory was pleased to call Pacific Coral and Russet Brown.

Reckoning from James Ward Packard's first car in 1899 to the end of production in 1958, Packard was one of the longest-lived firms in the industry and in its nearly six decades of production sent to the highways some of the noblest carriages the world has known. Its accomplishments were formidable. In 1919, a Packard held the Land Speed Record, at 149.8 miles an hour, Ralph de Palma driving, at Daytona Beach. More, even, than Cadillac, the Packard was the premier American status symbol; indeed, it was esteemed all over the world. There were custom Packards built that ran to $35,000, although the standard off-the-showroom floor price never exceeded $10,000. Heads of state bought armored Packards — one such was made for Franklin Roosevelt in 1938 — and their consorts indulged in such whimsies as having interiors done to match the pink of a slipper: the pleasure of an Indian maharani.

The Twin-Six Packard, one of the first twelve-cylinder motorcars, created, on its introduction in 1915, the most notable sensation the industry was to know until the Model A Ford came along. The 85-horsepower engine carried the then-radical aluminum pistons, and ran more quietly and smoothly than anything then on the U.S. market. (It was a Twin-Six, modified to turn out 110 horsepower, that De Palma used at Daytona.) Like Rolls-Royce, Packard loftily declined the annual model-change policy of lesser manufactories, secure in the conviction that it did not need to bother. In New York, Chicago, Boston, Los Angeles, Philadelphia and lesser communities across the land lovely custom bodies by Brunn, Dietrich, Darrin ran the boulevards. But the company stayed too long with the heavy iron, and the light and cheap Model 120, designed to accommodate itself to the Depression market, came too late. In 1954 Studebaker absorbed Packard, and the end of the road lay four years ahead.

RUXTON

Year: *1930*
Model: *Series C*
Cylinders: *8*
Horsepower: *100*
Price: *$3195*

Ruxton is one of those cars that become imbedded in the consciousness of motorcar connoisseurs, despite being so rare that few have ever seen one. The Squire, of England, is another such. It's not remarkable that few of us have seen a Ruxton; there were only 52 of them built in the two years the company existed, 1929 to 1931. The car was a product of the New Era Company, which absorbed Gardner, Kissel and Moon, and was striking for its time in being front-wheel-drive. This configuration allowed a very low floor, and the Ruxton was touted as being nearly a foot lower than anything else on the road. Front-wheel drive, while offering the very attractive flat-floor advantage, did not have full commercial acceptance until the Citroën came along in France, despite Cord, which was really only a *succès d'éstime*. The root-difficulty is of course in the fact that the driven wheels must steer, with consequent alteration of the caster angle; some f.w.d. cars will show both understeer and oversteer in the same bend, depending upon whether power is on or off. Early f.w.d. cars had frequent universal-joint failures, owing to speed changes between the driving and driven components in each revolution. In the 1966 Oldsmobile Toronado, General Motors engineers broke through two conventions previously held as gospel: that a f.w.d. car could not demonstrate neutral-steer in a bend regardless of throttle opening, and that f.w.d. could not handle a really big engine.

It was not inefficiency in its drive-line arrangements that sank the Ruxton with so big a trace, however. It was expensive for its time, some models running nearly to $5000; and it was radical, in an age when radical things weren't popular. The body was stamped from British Wolseley dies, by the way, and assembled by Budd in the United States. Appointments and upholstery were to a high standard, with color styling by the premier stage-designer of the time, Joseph Urban. At least one Ruxton sedan was done in horizontally striped rainbow colors, the bands 4 to 8 inches wide, from top to bottom of the car!

166

GARDNER

Year: *1930*
Model: *Series 150*
Cylinders: *8*
Horsepower: *126*
Price: *$2045*

Many collectors are wedded to the notion that only the so-called "great" cars are worth restoration and preservation, only automobiles of unusual beauty or performance or mechanical innovation, or cars that marked a turning point, like the Model T Ford or the Rolls-Royce Silver Ghost. The point is valid for specialist connoisseurs, but in a collection of the size and purpose of Harrah's it is not, for an attempt to illustrate the whole history of the automobile must find room for quite pedestrian makes that are important because they *were* pedestrian, and therefore typical. The Gardner was not an exciting automobile, and one authority has remarked that he was baffled by the Gardner slogan, "A Distinctively Different Motor

Car," because he was unable to discover in what particular it was different. It was made in St. Louis, this individual car one of two phaetons produced for the New York and Chicago shows of 1930. The original owner said he had had 94 miles an hour indicated out of it. An insurance policy that came with some Gardners *was* "distinctively different." Written by Lloyd's, it indemnified the owner against loss of the car by theft, at rate of five dollars a day for a maximum of thirty days. Not really a fortune, but, considering that it was free . . . Some few Gardners were built on Ruxton chassis carrying modified bodies and radiator shells. Gardner had held the original contract to build Ruxtons for the New Era Motor Company.

BENTLEY

Year: *1931*
Model: *8–Litre*
Cylinders: *6*
Horsepower: *225*
Price: *$13,000* (*est.*)

Three thousand and sixty-one Bentley cars were built in the life of the British company, which ran roughly from 1919 to 1930, and of these exactly one hundred were the 8-Litre model. An 8-Litre engine is big today (482 cubic inches, as against say 327 for a Chevrolet) but in the late 1920's it was huge. This example is unusual in having convertible coachwork; sedan or limousine bodies were more often fitted to the 8-Litre. The cost, depending on the body, was around $13,000.

Bentley sold 1639 of his famous 3-Litre cars, and, at the bottom of the list, fifty of the 4½-Litre supercharged model, which was a failure. Oddly, the 8-Litre, which sold only twice that number, was a remarkable commercial success. The market would have absorbed many more than a hundred of them, but at the peak of the demand the small factory was fully occupied with turning out the fifty 4½-Litre blown cars required as minimum production by the rules of the Le Mans 24-Hour Race. W. O. Bentley himself was in opposition to the plan, which was certainly a factor in the subse-

quent failure of the company, but he was outvoted.

The 8-Litre was built, like the Bentley Continental and other models in our own day, for privileged people. Only the wealthy could afford the car and only people who were significant, or thought themselves to be, could be comfortable in it. It was big, powerful and fast: it would run from 6 miles an hour to 104 in high gear alone, and W. O. Bentley drove an early model across France from Dieppe to Cannes in a single day without, as he has said, "having to turn the lights on." He left Dieppe early in the morning, and was in Cannes before dusk.

Some remarkable bodies were built on 8-Litre chassis The Nawab of Bhopal had a hunting car done by Thrupp & Maberly which must have been something to see, particularly at night, with all its nine forward-facing lights on. (Two of them were detachable, and had 100 yards of reeled cable apiece on the running board.) The car had four batteries, teak woodwork, two refrigerators and other useful amenities.

170

FORD

Year: *1931*
Model: *A*
Cylinders: *4*
Horsepower: *40*
Price: *$625*

The successor to the Model T ran from 1927 to 1932, and its introduction roused undreamt-of curiosity in the United States: in major cities from coast to coast, police were called out to control the crowds.

The Model A was a much more conventional car than the T — it even had a gearshift lever — but it was, like its great predecessor, practical, sturdy, and tremendous value for money. A Model A could be elegant, too, as this De Luxe Phaeton is, with its side-mounted tire, two-toned leather seats, matching top, and wood trunk-carrier. Like all soundly designed objects, it looked good when it was new, and it still does.

PIERCE-ARROW   *Regal!*

Year: *1931*
Model: *41*
Cylinders: *8*
Horsepower: *132*
Price: *$5375*

By 1931, time was running out for the Pierce-Arrow. It would be, perhaps, a victim of the company's obsession with quality, with near-perfection. The best in materials and, particularly, in manufacturing and inspection methods, was only just good enough. The Pierce-Arrow attracted perceptive buyers of unlimited means. The Shah Riza Khan of Persia paid $25,000 for a Pierce-Arrow. It had a gold-plated radiator and diamonds of suitable dimension, set here and there in the interior. (Gold-plating is not as profligate as it sounds. The late James Melton had a Pierce-Arrow touring limousine on a Packard chassis, a car that he had restored especially for his wife. All the hardware, inside and out, was gold-plated, and I remember his telling me that it had cost no more than first-class chromium. The car was very striking, the upholstery in coarse linen with a large floral pattern.) King Albert of the Belgians and Ibn Saud had Pierce-Arrows.

Where other big-car manufacturers, Ford and General Motors for example, balanced their top-line cars with cheaper, faster-selling, more profitable models, Pierce did not. The company also resisted, at first, the trend to multi-cylinder engines. Sales dropped frighteningly. In 1925, the company tried a gimmick: an all-aluminum car in cooperation with the Aluminum Company of America. The public wasn't ready. Studebaker bought the firm in 1928 and set about making a twelve-cylinder engine. In 1933, one of the greatest of all "last hope" cars appeared: the Pierce-Arrow "Silver Arrow." This was a masterwork, years ahead of its time. Wind-tunnel-formed, it really was streamlined, would reach 120 miles an hour on a 175-horsepower engine, an engine that ran in seven main bearings, and had hydraulic valve-lifters and an oil cooler. Power brakes were standard. The sedan body was strikingly good-looking, exciting without being unacceptably radical. But it cost $10,000 and the market wasn't there. When one thinks of the Pierce-Arrow one thinks, as perhaps one should, of the last of the regular line, cars like this Model 41 Custom Club Sedan, with the fender-faired headlights that were for so long the make's signature.

LINCOLN

Year: *1932*
Model: *KB*
Cylinders: *12*
Horsepower: *150*
Price: *$6400*

No one named Lincoln had anything to do with the Lincoln automobile, which was named after Abraham Lincoln by its creator, Henry M. Leland, a Vermonter who began his working life as a gunsmith during the Civil War. He moved to Detroit in 1890, set up a machine shop, and was head of Cadillac in 1903. When Cadillac was absorbed by General Motors, then in the hands of William Durant, Leland and his son went with it.

Everything Leland made, all his life, he tried to make to gunsmith's standards, and it was he who was responsible for Cadillac's winning the Dewar Trophy in 1908, when three Cadillacs were torn down and jumbled, 89 parts replaced by spares, then reassembled by mechanics using only hand tools and run for 500 miles. Leland made the first American V–8 engine, too, in 1914. (The actual first was probably De Dion–Bouton's in 1907.) But in 1917 he got into a policy dispute with Mr. Durant, which ended the way those things usually did: Leland left the company. He made Liberty engines during the war, and set up the Lincoln company immediately afterward. The first Lincolns were superior mechanically and disastrous in style. In 1922 the company was in receivership. Leland estimated its worth at $16,000,000 but the courts halved that, and Henry Ford bought it. The Lelands went with the deal, but the table of organization in the Ford Motor Company showed only one chief and many Indians, and within four months the Lelands resigned.

The Lincoln became Edsel Ford's concern, and he greatly reduced its manufacturing cost without lessening its quality. The KB model was the best of the Lincolns, a motorcar made to the most exacting standards. It was fast, quiet, long-lived. On the KB chassis Edsel Ford had bodies built by the custom coachmakers of the day, often in units of 100 for regular sale. An example of the standards he enforced: he would allow no woodwork made of jointed or steam-bent pieces; everything had to be cut from solid timber. This convertible sedan by Dietrich is typical of the Ford-built Lincolns.

BUGATTI

Year: *1932*
Model: *Type 50 T*
Cylinders: *8*
Horsepower: *200*
Price: *$14,000 (est.)*

The smallest Bugatti was called the Type 52 and was six feet long and powered by an electric motor. The original was made as a gift for Ettore Bugatti's younger son Roland, who was five at the time—1927. These toys, scale miniatures of the grand prix cars, were usually called Baby Bugattis and would do a brisk 12 miles an hour and stop themselves with four-wheel brakes. They would reverse, ran on pneumatic tires and weighed a stout 150 pounds.

Somewhere between the Baby and M. Bugatti's biggest car, the Royale, which measured rather more than 15 feet in wheelbase and sold, in bare chassis form without body, for $20,000, the Type 50 appears in line. The Type 50 is a nobly proportioned carriage, and the engine, supercharged to develop 200 horsepower, was almost awesomely strong for its time. The Type 50 was one of the few Bugatti models using a three-speed gearbox. Four was normal, but the low-speed torque of the 50 engine was so great that the extra gear was superfluous. The top speed was not high, theoretically 110 and actually perhaps 95, but at ordinary cruising speeds the engine was required to turn at only 3000 RPM or so, when lesser vehicles might be screaming along at 5000 to keep up with it. The

acceleration was of course formidable, and even today, a properly tuned Type 50 will not be embarrassed on the road. At about 2000 RPM, the supercharger begins to be heard, the sound rising to a pronounced sirenlike scream at 4000 or so, and drivers being passed have a tendency to scuttle to the side of the road, slowing, I think because they imagine that a fire engine or a police car is alongside. Most Bugattis appear to the driver to be light, lithe, nervous, catlike, requiring and rewarding management, but the Type 50 is a gentleman's carriage in the classic mode, moving majestically, yet capable of disputing a run down to a corner if the occasion arises.

Most Bugatti engines had a racing background, and the 50 engine was used in Type 53 and 54 grand prix cars, and in standard touring form a team of them ran in the 1931 Le Mans race. The cars were withdrawn when a burst tire put one of them off the circuit and killed a spectator.

There are seventeen Type 50's known to exist at the moment, and the Harrah Collection holds two of them— this one, its radically sloping windshield identifying the body as a *coupé profilé*, and the other a three-passenger coupé by the Paris coachmakers Million et Guiet.

178

DUESENBERG

Year: *1933*
Model: *SJ*
Cylinders: *8*
Horsepower: *320*
Price: *$15,000*

This is probably the newest, in the sense of being the least-used, of Duesenbergs. There were 1342 miles on the odometer when it came to the Harrah Collection. It is an SJ, the supercharged version of the Model J, running a centrifugal-type blower delivering air under a pressure of eight pounds per square inch. The first purchaser was Mr. George Whittell, of Tahoe, Nevada, who used the car little because he was disturbed by the public attention accompanying its appearance. Replacement of the rubber mat in the rumble-seat compartment was all that was required to put the car into as-new condition (mice had been at it!). Discovery of a desirable classic or antique stored for years in a hot dry climate is the hope of collectors, and one rarely fulfilled; this SJ had not only spent nearly three decades in such happy condition, but had in addition been carefully maintained and looked after.

The aluminum body was designed by Gordon Buehrig, who did the coffin-nosed Cord; fenders, lamps and bumpers are special, and the exhaust header was specially designed to allow a parallel escape lineup of the exposed pipes. The body is by Weymann.

To find a Duesenberg comparable with this, one would have to seek out the two short-chassis (125-inch) SJ's made to special order for Clark Gable and Gary Cooper, roadsters of an elegance that can be rated only with the long-lost two-seater Bugatti *Royale* crafted to Jean Bugatti's specifications.

A peculiarity of the Duesenberg mystique is the establishment, in Weston, Connecticut, called Hoe Sportcar. Here, in a garage that can accommodate only six cars, Arthur James Hoe repairs and restores Duesenbergs. They come to him from Hong Kong, from Buenos Aires, from Amsterdam. Of the 470 Model J's that were built in the lifetime of the company, Hoe has seen and held under his hand nearly 250. He may keep a car for six months, or eight; when he releases it, he does not expect to see it again for five years. He is, in my limited view, the best old-car mechanic in the Western world. His primary concern is to send the cars out of his shop shiny-bright, modified to run on today's gasoline, and flawless in every particular from hand-rubbed chassis to precisely focused taillight. Of all the automobiles we have known, only Bentley, Bugatti and Duesenberg can command such devotion from men of Hoe's stature.

AUSTIN

Year: *1933*
Model: *2-75*
Cylinders: *4*
Horsepower: *13*
Price: *$305*

Herbert Austin was one of the founding fathers of mass-motoring in Europe and the world. He designed his first car in 1895, while on the payroll of the Wolseley Sheep-Shearing Company, and set up his own company in 1906. (It became one of the biggest in Europe and in 1951 was the base factor in the merger that made British Motor Corporation.)

The first Austins were lumpy, heavy, but marvelously long-lasting big cars. They sold well, and the company prospered as they went, but it was the Austin Seven of 1922 that really shook up the British market. It was the first really small mass-produced car. Bugatti had made such a device for the Peugeot company before the Kaiser War, the "Bébé" Peugeot, but not many of them ever came to the roads, while something more than 250,000 Austin Sevens were made, a great number when the size of the British market of the time is considered. (By 1936 there was even a racing Seven, a tiny single-seater with a supercharged double-overhead-camshaft engine giving 116 horsepower and running at 12,000 revolutions a minute!) Spidery and frail-looking, the Austin Seven was actually a fairly sturdy little machine, had four-wheel brakes from the beginning — they had minuscule drums and were inefficient, but that didn't matter, the car wouldn't go fast anyway — and could be made to deliver 60 miles on an Imperial gallon of gasoline.

It was from this root that the American Austin, later the Bantam, developed. Incredibly cheap, the Austin was well-made, adequate transportation in every particular, and great value for money. It would do about 50 miles an hour. A hazard involved in the Bantam was that three strong teen-agers, catching one at a stoplight, could pick up the rear end, thus immobilizing it. The idea was to hope the driver would spin the wheels in rage. If he did, he was dropped, and thus, if a half-shaft didn't go, achieved a very quick takeoff.

BREWSTER

Year: *1934*
Model: *Not designated*
Cylinders: *8*
Horsepower: *90*
Price: *$3500*

The idea that originated the Brewster was simplicity itself: in the middle 1930's, when Franklin Delano Roosevelt was rampant in the land, and the real rich were convinced that the best they could hope for was confiscation of all their worldly goods (they hoped that their wives and daughters would be spared, though they doubted it), it seemed the course of wisdom not to rouse the beasts, not to infuriate the proles with wanton display of goods. It was prudent, one heard on Vanderbilt Avenue and on 44th Street and Lower Park Avenue, in the warm leather-bound comfort of the Yale Club, the Harvard Club, the New York Yacht Club, the Union League, to put the Rolls-Royce, the Hisso, the Isotta on blocks. Horrid tales were floating in the land, of gentry bombarded with perished tomatoes, turnips, beets, eggs past other usefulness, and even bricks, while coaching along the avenues in their ordinary, $10,000 go-to-meeting imported vehicles. So, under the necessity of the times, an inspiration struck the Brewsters, longtime Rolls-Royce specialists and coachbuilders to the quality. Why not put a sumptuous town-car body on the most plebeian chassis available, namely, the Ford? Little sooner said than done. The end product was handsome. From without, that is to say, from the point of view of the brickthrower, the barricade-destroyer, it was comparatively inoffensive. But, within, it could be as luxurious as one wished. Cheap, too: $3500 would buy the basic Brewster, and thus it served the genuine needs of tycoons temporarily impoverished. The Brewster was a town car, a true coupé-de-ville, with the chauffeur out-of-doors, exposed, as befitted his station, to the various inclemencies. (He did, however, have a convertible covering at his disposal in case of Force 8 storms.) A footman was not usually carried.

MORGAN

Year: *1934*
Model: *Super Sports*
Cylinders: *2*
Horsepower: *40*
Price: *$660*

Automobiles have been built with two wheels, three, four, six, eight, but of the odd-numbered designs, only three-wheelers have been made in any quantity (there are several in being today) and the Morgan is the best known of all.

The Morgan Three-Wheeler came into being in 1911, creature of a notably individualistic Englishman, Henry Frederick Stanley Morgan. About 40,000 Three-Wheelers were made, in not very many variants, most of them from 1911 to 1939, although they were still available to special order as late as 1953. They were taxed as motorcycles in Great Britain, and this, plus their running economy (up to 90 miles to the Imperial gallon!) made them an attractive financial proposition. They were very light—some models weighed only 550 pounds—and with a 50-horsepower engine to hurry them along, they were quick. Racing Morgans would do over 100 miles an hour, and drivers whose ambitions to get into competition were backed by thin bank accounts found them nearly irresistible.

The Three-Wheeler was an acquired taste, nevertheless. The ride was harsh. Until 1926 they had no brakes on the front wheels, and to brake the single rear wheel at 80 miles an hour was an endeavor more academic than practical. There were only two pedals on the floor, clutch and brake. The accelerator was a lever in the steering wheel, and Morgan drivers were forever amusing each other with tales of catching the throttle in a coat sleeve, or forgetting, when turning the wheel, that up was now on and down off instead of the other way around. The throttle had no return spring. When it was turned on, it stayed on. Morgans had a button-down fabric top, but no doors (one climbed over) and not many had self-starters fitted to the big two-cylinder motorcycle engine hung out in front of the radiator, standard until after World War II. This combination of circumstances made stalling the engine in traffic on a wet day most unusually embarrassing, particularly if there were no passengers aboard to work the throttle and spark levers in the event the thing *did* start on the crank.

Men liked them a lot better than women did, as a rule, but the all-time speed record for a Morgan Three-Wheeler (it was an international motorcycle record until a few years ago) was made in the 1930's by a woman, Gwenda Stewart Hawkes, at 116 miles an hour. She also ran one at 101 MPH for an hour, and at 72 MPH for twelve consecutive hours. Mrs. Hawkes was held by her male contemporaries to be a very brave and very strong young lady.

CHRYSLER

Year: *1935*
Model: *Airflow Imperial*
Cylinders: *8*
Horsepower: *130*
Price: *$1475*

The Airflow model by Chrysler set up a great stir when it appeared and has been argued over ever since. It is probably the most-discussed failure of all time.

Failure of the Airflow model did much to convince Detroit of the supreme importance of body design, or "styling," because the car was advanced in concept and soundly made. It should have been a big seller, but as a commercial proposition it was sunk without a trace because the buying public didn't like the look of the thing. It has been a cliché ever since 1935, when it was introduced, to say that the Airflow Chrysler failed because it was too far ahead of its time. This view has been disputed by authorities of the stature of Gordon Buehrig, who did the bodies for the 810 and 812 Cords: the car was ugly when it was built, Buehrig has said, and it's ugly now, and that is why it failed. Designed by Carl Breer, one of Chrysler's original associates, the model was built on a 146-inch wheelbase, but was 10 inches wider than the Custom Im-

perial Eight that had preceded it. Weight distribution was altered from 40/60 front/rear to 55/45 and the suspension was softened. The wheels were well-placed as near to the corners of the car as possible, to spare the passengers some road-shock — to "cradle" them, as Chrysler people put it — and luxuries such as silent transmission gears embodying free-wheeling, and a vacuum clutch, were specified. The body was meant to reflect the growing knowledge of aerodynamics, but it was not really streamlined, as a wind-tunnel-grown body would have been, and it was esthetically as wrong as could be. The split windshield looked wrong, the radiator line was bulbous and the fender treatment seemed almost certainly to have been an afterthought. Mechanically it was a splendid motorcar, but it didn't look the part, and the public would have none of it. The biggest of the Airflows, the CW, sold fewer than 100 copies. Chrysler wrote it off and went on to bigger and better things.

LINCOLN ZEPHYR

Year: *1936*
Model: *H*
Cylinders: *12*
Horsepower: *110*
Price: *$1320*

The KB Lincoln was *succeeded* by the Model K and KA cars, which had smaller engines and were not, and were not meant to be, up to the standards of the KB's. There was a depression on, and everybody making big luxury automobiles felt the squeeze. Companies that had other strings to their bows, like Rolls-Royce and General Motors and Ford, could manage, but single-make firms dropped like flies. A Briggs body designer named John Tjaarda worked out a rear-engine medium-size car and it was shown to Edsel Ford, who liked it a great deal. Henry Ford was apt to be set in his ways, slow to be excited by something new, reluctant to change. For example, like Ettore Bugatti, another dedicated individualist, he resisted hydraulic brakes for years, believing that brakes should be applied by linkages of solid metal, that trying to stop a two-ton motorcar with oil squirted through a rubber hose was, on the face of it, a spectacularly bad idea. But Edsel, like Jean Bugatti, was progressive in outlook, and although Ford production and management people emphatically rejected the radicalism of a rear-engine car, it was decided to rework the design for front-engine manufacture and bring it out as a realistically priced Lincoln. Actually, the Lincoln Zephyr was not a small Lincoln, it was a big Ford; it was not a good-looking car and it made no great splash in the market. It developed into a steady seller, nonetheless, and it notched up two important advances: it was the first "unitized" or frameless body to be put into American production, made so that the body itself was a stressed, load-carrying component, instead of being just a separate structure dropped onto the chassis, and it was the first Ford product to be created by a department of designers, rather than one man. (Tjaarda's original design had of course been radically modified.) This began the Detroit trend to design by committee which, for good or ill, is still the way it's done today. The Zephyr also has a place as the immediate antecedent of the great Lincoln Continental, which began life as Edsel's personal car and went into production when it became obvious that everyone who saw it wanted it.

190

MASERATI

Year: *1936*
Model: *6CM*
Cylinders: *6*
Horsepower: *280/310*
Price: *$8500*

The Maserati of Italy has the distinction of being the only foreign car to win twice in succession at Indianapolis since World War I. A Maserati won the 500 in 1939 and 1940, the legendary Wilbur Shaw driving. As Indianapolis custom dictates, it was not called a Maserati, but a "Bowes Seal-Fast Special," after the Chicago firm sponsoring it. It was a veritable Maserati, nevertheless, a creation of the four Maserati brothers, Alfieri, Bindo, Ettore and Ernesto, who formed the company in 1925 and maintained it until 1946.

Racing motorcars, straight and simple, interested the Maserati brothers more than anything else, and they were fierce competitors on the world's circuits. Of course they made sports cars as well, for competitive use, and high-performance passenger cars. One of their sports cars was notable: the model "Sedici cilindri" of 1932. This two-seater had an engine configuration not often encountered: two supercharged eight-cylinder engines side by side. (Ettore Bugatti did the same thing in his Type 47 grand prix car.) The car was a handful to drive, but those who could manage it in the corners were rewarded by speeds over 150 miles an hour on the straights. Few were made, but at least one example survives.

This Maserati is a Tipo 6 CM, a single-seat racing car designed to run in the "voiturette" class in the 1930's. This car, in the hands of Count Carlo Trossi, won at the Nürburgring in 1936, and another Maserati was second to it. Its color, incidentally, would identify it as Italian on any European race circuit. Separate colors were long ago assigned to countries which support race cars—including some, like Thailand, which support rather few. Bright red is Italy's color, silver is for Germany, blue for France, yellow for Belgium, white-and-blue for the United States, green for Great Britain. (The British green has never been standardized, but *any* car, painted *any* shade of green, is sure, in an advertisement for sale, to carry the cryptic initials BRG for British Racing Green.) I have never seen an Egyptian race car, but I should like to: it would be painted pale violet with red numbers.

CORD

Year: *1937*
Model: *812 Supercharged*
Cylinders: *8*
Horsepower: *170*
Price: *$2745*

Gordon Buehrig, who designed the body and the interior of the Model 810/812 Cord in 1934–1935, to this day treasures one remark made about the car: "It looks as if it had been born on the road and grew up there."

Taking every care to avoid unwarranted superlatives, still it must be said that this was one of the happiest arrangements of mass and line ever to come off an automobile stylist's drawing board. It was radical, and years ahead of its time, but it was instantly recognized as nearly perfect not only by connoisseurs but by laymen. The thousands of visitors to the New York Automobile Show in November 1935, where the Cord was first shown, were polled, asked to cite three choices for the best-looking car on the floor. The Cord drew more votes than the second and third place cars together. In 1949 the Museum of Modern Art in New York City cited the 810/812 Cord as one of the ten best designs, and an as-new Cord is worth more today than it was when production stopped in 1937.

Oddly, the car resulted from compromise in a dozen directions. The first intention was to call it a Duesenberg, and make it smaller and cheaper than the standard Duesenbergs, on an Auburn chassis. The project was dropped for six months, then revived as a crash program, at a time when the resources of the Auburn-Cord-Duesenberg company amounted to less than a million dollars, a circumstance that dictated improbable and desperate improvisations in production. There was no time for proper testing, and the first delivered models annoyed their owners by such nuisances as overheating and jumping out of gear. Priced at $2000–$3000 when big Buicks went for $895, the Cord was a luxury car in a depression market. In all, only about three thousand were made, but the impact of those few was so strong that in 1965 it was thought feasible to undertake the manufacture of a replica, very slightly smaller, but otherwise an exact copy in styling. (The technological advances of thirty years naturally dictated mechanical changes.)

The Cord was full of innovation. A V–8 Lycoming engine drove the front wheels. A supercharger was optional. It had no running boards and a step-down floor. The headlights retracted under faired flaps, as the Buick Riviera's did thirty years later. The convertible sedan was the first true four-passenger convertible, and the top, although manually controlled, disappeared completely when down. It was a fast motorcar, roadable and beautiful in very nearly unique proportions.

JAGUAR

Year: *1937*
Model: *SS–100*
Cylinders: *6*
Horsepower: *125*
Price: *$1925*

The Jaguar, one of the topmost postwar successes, descends from this SS–100, and through it from the original SS–1 of 1932. The SS (the initials have no meaning, not Standard Swallow or Swallow Sports or Special Standard or Swallow Special or any of the other tags usually put on them) was the first creation of William Lyons, now Sir William Lyons, and it appeared at the Olympia Motor Show in London in October 1931. Lyons had a tiny six-man company called Swallow Coach Building which made motorcycle sidecars at the beginning and then branched out to make special bodies for the small cars of the period: Austin, Fiat, Standard and so on. A Standard chassis and engine were used for the first SS, and on this chassis was erected a stunning coupé body, the bonnet actually considerably longer than the body (excluding the trunk) and very low. It was the sensation of the Olympia Show, and no one imagined, on first seeing it, that it would be sold for a mere $1500. It was underpowered, but it *looked* absolutely wonderful, and Lyons took immediate action in the matter of power. A new six-cylinder engine went in, and the SS–90 and SS–100 models (the numerals refer to top speed) would in fact produce the advertised figures. In the middle 1930's the name Jaguar was added, and the cars were known as SS Jaguars until the Hitler War, when the initials SS became anathema. During the war, when they had a few hours, Jaguar engineers, particularly W. M. Heynes, worked on the engine which was to drive the extraordinary XK–120, a high-performance six-cylinder, twin-overhead-camshaft design that was to be most amazingly long-lived—it is still basically the Jaguar engine.

Like the great prewar Bentleys, the Jaguars had a fabulous streak of wins at Le Mans, in 1951, 1953, 1955, 1956 and 1957. The 4.2 model is one of the world's great sedans today and the E–type two-seater, a 150–MPH motorcar, offers performance comparable with Aston-Martin or Ferrari two-seaters at less than half the cost. To produce motorcars giving exceptional value for money has been William Lyons's basic purpose from the beginning.

BUGATTI

Year: *1937*
Model: *Type 57*
Cylinders: *8*
Horsepower: *135*
Price: *$6500*

This coach carries Ettore Bugatti's own bodywork, in the style called Galibier. It's typical of the elegant passenger vehicles he produced when he was at the peak of his powers, when possession of one of his cars certified one's taste and affluence, as possession of a Ferrari does today. (Sometimes the wish to acquire a Bugatti testified to other things: a young lady of Paris confessed that she had killed her father because he had refused her money with which to buy a Bugatti for her lover!)

The Type 57 was mechanically straightforward enough, by Bugatti standards, meant to be a fast touring car, refined and quiet, no demi-racer, as were some other models out of the Molsheim factory. It was probably the best of the passenger Bugattis, and comparatively a large number were made, probably around 750 in the five years from 1934 to 1939. The design reflected thinking by Bugatti's older son, Jean, a brilliant young man who would very much have liked to race his father's cars, but was forbidden. He died just before the beginning of World War II while testing a car on a road he thought to be empty, and which in fact was empty except for a mailman, bicycle-mounted and the worse for wine. Jean Bugatti lost control of the car avoiding him, and rolled it.

The Galibier Type 57 cost $6500, a serious sum of money in 1937, but the customer got for his money distinction, elegance and mechanical refinement. The engine was of double-overhead-camshaft configuration, as any really high-performance engine must be, and it had years of development engineering behind it. It can be said of Bugatti, as it has been said of Enzo Ferrari, that he really made only one engine, but never stopped working on it. This is one of the marks of all great motorcars: years of concentration on a single superior design. One thinks of Rolls-Royce, Porsche, Ferrari, Ford.

Bugatti made three important variations on the Type 57 theme: Types 57S, 57C, 57SC, in ascending order of performance value; the 57SC a supercharged sports version usually in coupé form, and capable of 125 MPH, a really extraordinary rate of travel for a passenger automobile in 1939. The coupé model Atlantic was bizarre indeed, a sloped-back hardtop of very light Electron alloy, seamed and riveted over the front mudguards, seamed and riveted over the center roofline, the windshield in two parts as well, the dashboard very fully instrumented, with about a foot and a half of polished steering-post bringing the wheel to the driver's hands.

HISPANO-SUIZA

Year: *1938*
Model: *K-6*
Cylinders: *6*
Horsepower: *120*
Price: *$12,500 (est.)*

"Hispano-Suiza" has a marvelously romantic ring, but all it means is "Spanish-Swiss." Marc Birkigt, one of the half-dozen great originators in the world of the motorcar, was a Swiss, and his financial backers in the manufacture of his first automobile were Spanish, and so it came about. Early Hispano-Suiza cars were made in Barcelona, later ones in Paris. The four-cylinder *voiturette* of 1909, later called the Alfonso XIII after the King of Spain, a light, graceful, quick little car, was Birkigt's first success. It was the beginning of a long procession, for he was talented and versatile. During World War I he made airplane engines, more than fifty thousand of them. In this circumstance originated the silver-plated flying stork radiator emblem that so distinguished all postwar Hissos. Captain Georges Guynemer, one of the great French flying aces, had used the stork of Lorraine as his personal insignia, flying in Hisso-engined SPAD fighters, and Birkigt adopted the stork emblem in memory of him.

This Hispano-Suiza is a contemporary of the twelve-cylinder car usually thought of as Birkigt's masterwork. Some connoisseurs believe the Hispano-Suiza to be the finest motorcar of all time, with only the Rolls-Royce to be compared with it. (The famous Rolls-Royce wheel-locking system, by the way, was made under license from Hispano-Suiza.) The great Hissos were not only fast, even by today's standards, but luxurious, quiet, and made to standards impossible for anyone to achieve or afford today. (To settle a dispute about the quality of workmanship in the engine, a Hispano-Suiza was driven flat-out from Paris to Nice to Paris and run into the showroom window over a sheet of white paper. People stood around waiting for oil to drop. Legend insists none did.) An Australian reported a few years ago that his 1921 model had run 768,584 miles without a cylinder rebore and still did not show any sign of needing one! Michael Arlen's "The Green Hat," that period-piece of the 1920's, was only the most-quoted of many stories citing the Hispano-Suiza as a desirable and romantic possession.

GRAHAM

Year: *1938*
Model: *Supercharged Series 97*
Cylinder: *6*
Horsepower: *116*
Price: *$1598*

The supercharged automobile has always been an American rarity, although the device originated in this country, on the Chadwick, made in Philadelphia in 1907, and lifted the speed of the car to 100 miles an hour. It was probably the first production-line car that would touch three figures.

The supercharger is an air-pump, and its purpose is simple enough: to force more air-and-fuel mixture into the cylinders than ordinary induction—the suction-effect of the descending pistons—can bring in. It "charges" the cylinders, in other words, beyond their normal capacity, thus supercharger. There are three basic forms: the Roots-type (invented in Indiana) which traps air between two figure-eight lobes and forces it into the engine; the vane-type, which is an adaptation of the paddle-wheel principle, and the centrifugal, which is a turbine-wheel. The Roots and vane-types, which run at engine speed or a little faster, are most efficient for varying-speed engines; the centrifugal, which must run very fast indeed, up to 40,000 revolutions a minute in some cases, is best for constant-speed engines such as aircraft types. Still, the Duesenberg used a centrifugal blower, and so did the 1934 Graham. A supercharger will increase the power of an engine—and the stresses imposed on it as well—and also lift its revolutions-per-minute capacity. The Graham-Paige, later the Graham, was a solid, standard go-to-meeting kind of car until 1932, when a long-wheelbase eight-cylinder model was catalogued, and in 1934 an aluminum-head supercharged engine cited at 135 horsepower came out. As in the Duesenberg, the blower was mounted on the right side of the engine, and while not useful in acceleration—centrifugal superchargers never are—it improved middle-ground performance and top speed, at some cost in gasoline consumption. The 1935 Series 110 Graham would do 112 miles an hour, a rate beyond the driving capability of most owners of the day. No American-built car comes with a supercharger as standard equipment today, although it is optional on the Chevrolet Corvair, but there are excellent proprietary makes available as "bolt-on" accessories for many sports cars and light sedans.

ALFA-ROMEO

Year: *1938*
Model: *8C2900B*
Cylinders: *8*
Horsepower: *220*
Price: *$11,000*

Alfa-Romeo is one of the hallowed names in international automobilism, and with very good reason. From 1909 to this moment, the firm has turned out vehicles superior in performance, beautiful in appearance and remarkable in longevity. Alfa-Romeo's racing record is high on the list of the most formidable, and one must agree with Ralph Stein that in the three decades before the Hitler War, in originality and elegance only Bugatti stands its peer.

Alfa-Romeo grew out of the enterprise of Alexandre Darracq, the French pioneer, who established two assembly plants in Italy, one in Naples and one in Milan, in 1906. Neither did well, and three years later they were taken over by an Italian company and the merged firm titled Anonima Lombardo Fabbrica Automobili, or A.L.F.A. In 1909 a young and brilliant engineer, Nicola Romeo, was brought in by the banks to reorganize the firm, thus Alfa-Romeo. Milan was made the center of activity, accounting for the Alfa-Romeo radiator badge: the snake symbol of the Crusaders from Milan, with the cross symbolic of the delivery of Jerusalem. From the beginning until 1949, when the firm's interest in racing began to decline, Alfa won 216 primary events, as against 170 for Bugatti and 117 for Mercedes, and placed a total of 560 times! The design and the finish of Alfa-Romeo engines was of such excellence that even the close-mouthed Henry Ford, never lavish in his estimates of foreign, or even domestic competitive, machinery once said, "I take my hat off when I see an Alfa-Romeo go by."

The engineer Vittorio Jano was responsible for most of Alfa's soaring designs, including the classic 1750-cc. car of 1929 which won every race in which it was entered that year: the Grands Prix of Belgium, Ireland, Monza, Rome, Spain, Tunis, the 24 Hours of Brooklands, the Mille Miglia, and the Ulster Tourist Trophy.

In 1935 the Nazi-supported Mercedes-Benz and Auto-Union teams began their crushing domination of grand prix racing, and the current Alfa-Romeo first-line competition car was, with the best of the British and French makes, outclassed. Thirty-six G.P. engines, now obsolete, were on hand, and Jano decreed that they be suitably detuned and put into road cars. This was the Tipo 8C2900B across the page: a twin-supercharged, independent-front-suspension sports car of the first order. Who could afford one bought it on sight: Michael of Rumania and Bernhard of Holland, to name two.

MERCEDES-BENZ

Year: *1938*
Model: *540K*
Cylinders: *8*
Horsepower: *115/180*
Price: *$9500*

Only about three hundred 540K's were built in 1937 and 1938, and while they were impressive machines, in a bulbous Teutonic fashion, and well made indeed, all the screw-slots line up, *und so weiter*, they were not distinguished for performance. A top speed of around 100 miles an hour was available to the 500K and 540K line, which was, after all, in 1938 — and is now — quite adequate for ordinary highway usage. The 540K here shown was suspended in an advanced fashion, independently front and rear on coil springs. The supercharger worked on the standard Mercedes-Benz principle, blowing through the carburetor with what is usually, among "enthusiasts," called a banshee* howl much esteemed by non-owners, or owners three or four times removed. It is doubtful if a review of all the self-advertising devices ever buttoned into a motorcar, from the Octoauto's four extra wheels to the Rolls-Royce's loud-tick clock, would turn up anything so effective, statuswise. Mercedes-Benz used this system because the engine was not stressed to accept standard, continuous supercharging, as in the contemporary Type 50 Bugatti, for example. The Mercedes blower was a "sprint" device. The idea was to use it in 10- or 15-second bursts, solely to build up speed, which could then be held, in the ordinary way of things, with the normally aspirated effort of the engine. However, as a touring car, which was what the thing was meant to be, a 540K was a satisfying device, comfortable, controllable and eminently reliable. It went like a moving house. It should have: it weighed nearly three tons. There was alleged to have been a 580K — I say "alleged" only because I never saw one — and about eighteen examples were built of the Grosser 770K, reserved for eminences of the Nazi Party. I once drove a 770K in Chicago; it was said, on dubious authority, to have been Der Fuehrer's personal car, indeed it may have been, for the window glass was an inch thick and the body was Krupp armor-plated. It had five speeds forward, the positions engraved on an ivory gearshift knob, lamentable acceleration, and hopelessly inadequate brakes, but at about 75 miles an hour, running on a straight line, it was one of the most comfortable vehicles I have ever known.

---

*BANSHEE: Spirit supposed by Irish and Highland superstition to wail under the windows of a house in which one of the inmates is about to die (*Oxford Illustrated Dictionary*).

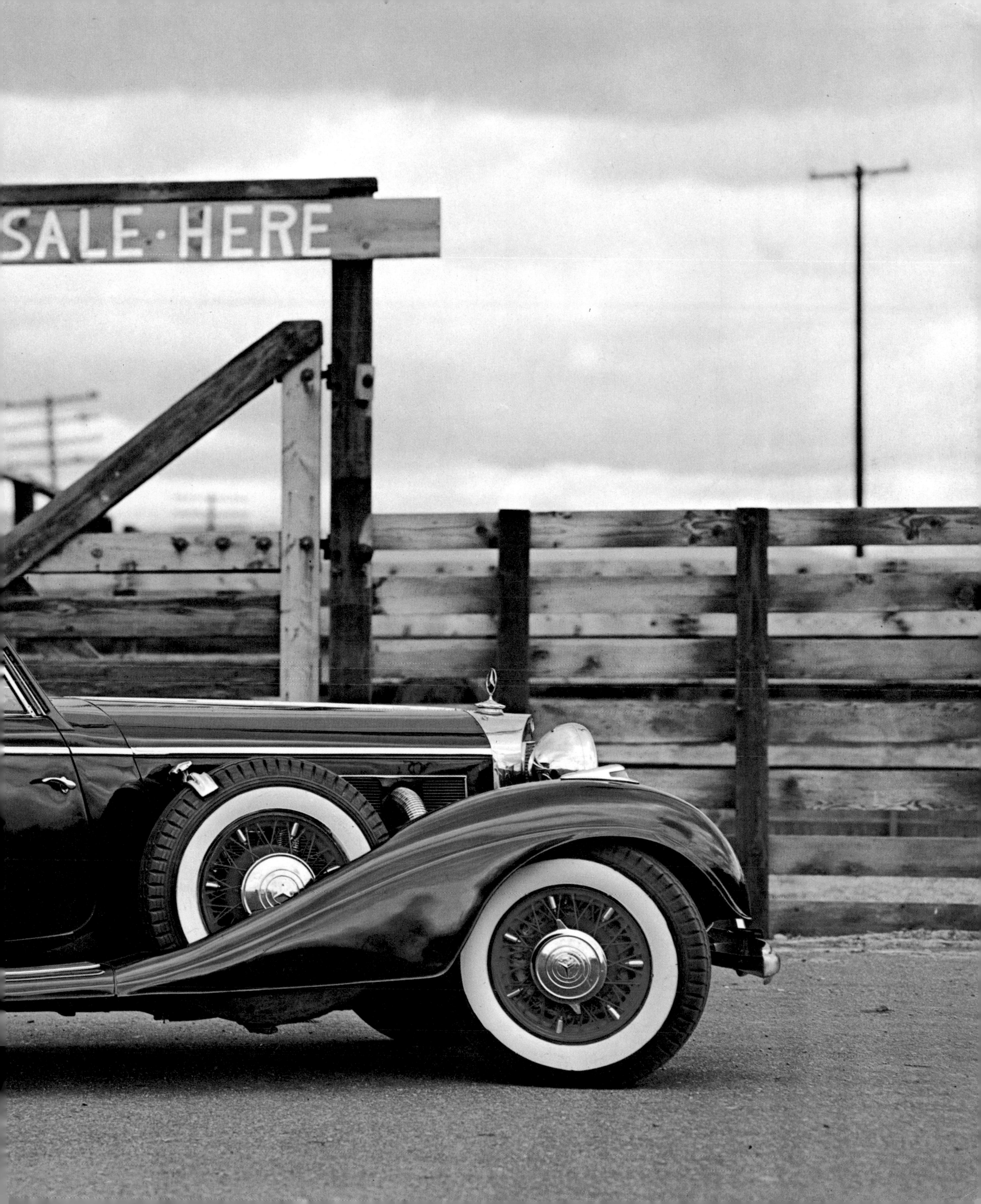
SALE·HERE

ROLLS-ROYCE

Year: *1938*
Model: *Phantom III*
Cylinders: *12*
Horsepower: *165*
Price: *$22,750*

More custom-built bodies have been erected on Rolls-Royce chassis, I am sure, than on any other, and probably three or four times as many, but I have never seen one combining elegance and grace with as much dash as does this *coupé de ville* by Franay of Paris. Here is a true town car, $22,750 expended on the transportation of two people. The crew were not as much unprotected as here appears. A top to cover the front compartment is carried in the trunk.

The chassis is the Phantom III, new in 1937, powered by the only 12-cylinder engine Rolls-Royce has put into a motorcar. (All the great Royces before the P-III carried six-cylinder engines; the present P-V is an eight.) On first experience of it, many Rolls-Royce devotees believed there could never be a better example, and perhaps they were right, although in its day, the Silver Ghost model was no doubt a better car than the Phantom III in its time. But on the P-III everything seemed to have been lavished. It was built like a Rolls-Royce, which is to say in the most craftsmanlike manner, of the best procurable material, and to last. It had all the old things, the power brakes for example, the force of their application precisely proportioned to the speed of the car, the foot-controlled chassis lubricator that sent metered amounts of oil to all chassis points, and there were brand-new refinements as well: one, the four built-in hydraulic jacks, controlled from the driver's seat, a device with which the tinny bumper jacks most luxury cars carry today compare unfavorably. The vehicle would do 100 miles an hour.

For a long span of years, certainly for thirty years, the Rolls-Royce claim to the title "The Best Car in the World" was justified. When only hand-fitting, infinite patience and disdain for cost would bring an automobile to the border of perfection, nothing else on wheels could consistently compare with the Derby product. But technology has made craftsmanship obsolete, and it's true that Ford today can produce, at the rate of one every 53 seconds, a car quieter than Rolls-Royce — an admirable feat, indeed, and not the less so because it has taken half a century to accomplish.

INDEX

213